The Bear

The Bear:

The Legendary Life of Coach Paul "Bear" Bryant

By Don Keith

Based on a screenplay by Al Browning, Jr.

CUMBERLAND HOUSE

NASHVILLE, TENNESSEE

The Bear: The Legendary Life of Coach Paul "Bear" Bryant
Published by Cumberland House Publishing
431 Harding Industrial Drive
Nashville, TN 37211

Library of Congress Cataloging-in-Publication Data

Keith, Don, 1947-
  The Bear : the life and times of Paul "Bear" Bryant / Don Keith.
      p. cm.
  ISBN-13: 978-1-58182-562-6 (hardcover : alk. paper)
  ISBN-10: 1-58182-562-5 (hardcover : alk. paper)
  1. Bryant, Paul W. 2. Football coaches--United States--Biography. I. Title.
  GV939.B79K45 2006
  796.332092--dc22
  [B]

                                                              2006016587

Printed in the United States
1 2 3 4 5 6 7 — 12 11 10 09 08 07 06

Contents

Author's Note

Few people knew bigger-than-life college football coach Bear Bryant better than sportswriter and columnist Al Browning. Browning covered Alabama Crimson Tide football for ten years while at The Tuscaloosa News, but their relationship was more than just journalist/coach. They were friends, as well, and that gave Browning a unique view of the man, especially in Bryant's final years before his retirement and untimely death a short while later.

Still, Browning did not rely totally on his own memory when he wrote about Bryant. He put together an excellent book, based partly on his own experiences with Bear, but primarily on the recollections of those who knew Coach Bryant even better than he did. It was titled I Remember Paul "Bear" Bryant: Personal Memories of College Football's Most Legendary Coach As Told by the People Who Knew Him Best. He also produced and marketed a video that contained on-camera reminiscences from many of those same people.

Of course, there have also been biographies that told the story of this amazing man from various perspectives (and an autobiography that included the coach's own view), as well as other works that focused on particular parts of Bryant's career, his coaching methods and his philosophy. While each of these books has added to the portrait of the man, we recently learned that there was yet another attempt to document the coach's life.

Before his own death in 2002, Al Browning completed a screenplay based on Bryant's life that he hoped would be produced as a theatrical feature or as a television mini-series. Much of the material in the script was drawn from the interviews he conducted for the book and video mentioned above, but some of it came from his own conversations with Bear, as the coach reminisced about growing up, starting his coaching career and becoming a true legend in the sport of college football.

Browning's screenplay has not yet been picked up for production. However, we were convinced that the material should be shared with everyone, just as Al hoped it someday would be. We felt that the best way to do that was to take Al's screenplay and develop it as a "novelization" of the scenes and events he wrote about, many of which Al personally witnessed or learned about directly from the people who did.

We hope that we have done Al's material justice. We also hope that you will learn more about the nature of the man through this effort, whether you are a longtime fan or a member of an entire new generation that never had the opportunity to hear that thunderous voice and the sudden cry of, "Bingo! That's a goody!" when a player passed an especially hard lick during game replays on his weekly television show.

Now, a brief word on what this book is not. As you will see, it is not an attempt to tell it all or to compile a definitive biography. Much of the material has appeared before and has been told from various perspectives. We do think this book serves as validation and clarification of those various recollections and, in some cases, a correction of inaccuracies.

Furthermore, it is not an exhaustive account of the man's life or a game-by-game recount of Bryant's remarkable career. Those works have been done before, as well.

This is, rather, a book that takes a different slant and comes from a unique viewpoint. It is one we hope adds to the understanding of the man and why he was so successful at what he did, and especially how he was able to positively affect so many people during his lifetime.

"I just have a talent for finding the heart of a football team," he once admitted, and it was certainly true.

Note, too, that we pull no punches. Al's screenplay dealt with some of the not so flattering aspects of the coach's life. So does this book. But we, as Al did, believe that these foibles only make the man more human, more real, and add to the accuracy of this material.

The publisher and author would like to thank Stacy Browning, Al's widow, for her generous help in making this material available to readers.

We would also like to acknowledge the efforts of Brad Edwards, who has been a part of ESPN television's and ESPN.com's coverage of college football for many years. His corrections and fact-finding have made this book much more readable and as accurate as it can be, considering the passage of time and the dimming memories of many of those involved in its events.

Certainly, some of the stories in this book are already known to those who closely followed Coach Bryant's career. However, there is much in Al's work and in the perspective of those he talked with in preparation for writing his screenplay that gives us a clearer picture of a man for whom winning was not the most important thing.

It was the only thing.

Don Keith
Indian Springs Village, Alabama

The Bear

Prologue

The Columnist has never seen anything like it. Five city blocks filled with mourners in a town of less than 85,000 souls. Three churches utilized for the funeral. Representatives of every major medium – local and national – on hand to chronicle the event.

From a distance, he thinks, it looks almost like a pep rally. But there are no cheers this day. No yell leaders. No blocks being made or passes being thrown or touchdowns being scored.

A gray hearse is parked at an angle in front of First United Methodist Church of Tuscaloosa. A black limousine and four buses are lined up just behind, all arranged inside barricades that keep the throng back from the church steps. But the crowd is not surging. It remains orderly…eerily quiet…as if the people are straining to catch any bit of sound that might escape from the big building.

Fifty thousand people, the police would estimate. All to pay their last respects to a man bigger than life. To Paul "Bear" Bryant, a football coach.

It's January 28, 1983, and the bright sun belies the somber mood of all who are gathered there. The Columnist shares that mood as he inches closer, watching, trying to record it all in his head. Hopefully, one day he can describe this scene as it plays out, telling it better than the TV cameras or the other reporters can.

The front doors of the church eventually open, and the strains of organ music drift outside on the gentle breeze. A minister in full robes emerges from the darkness inside into the anomalous cheer of the sunlight. Two associates follow him closely. They slowly make their way down the stacked steps. Eight young men come next, each one of them powerfully muscular with thick necks and short haircuts, appearing uncomfortable in their suits. They are carrying an ornate casket out the church house doorway and down the steep steps. The coffin is covered with a blanket of red and white carnations. Other than the sun, these flowers are the only brightness in the picture on this day.

Next comes the widow, Mary Harmon Bryant, short and thin, yet appearing much younger than her sixty-eight years. She wears a long, black dress with a veil and is flanked by two more football players, who escort her from the church toward the waiting limousine.

The Columnist watches along with the rest of the crowd, standing quietly and respectfully as the coach's son, Paul Bryant Jr., and his wife follow his mother. The coach's daughter, Mae Martin Tyson, is next with her husband. Then the coach's bodyguard and long-time friend, Billy Varner… a teenager, Marc Tyson, Bear's beloved grandson… two younger girls, also grandchildren of the coach. It is so quiet that the scuffs of their feet and tapping of their high heels on the pavement can be clearly heard from where The Columnist observes the scene, trying not to miss even the slightest nuance.

All of them stand aside, watching, as the eight young men slide the casket into the back of the hearse, handling their profound load as if it doesn't weigh more than an ounce. But the looks on the football players' faces show differently. Their burden is heavy indeed.

As the door of the hearse is shut, there are sobs from the crowd. Some turn away, unable to watch.

From the church doorway, a steady stream of football players pour out, many with handkerchiefs at the ready…some openly weeping, all somber-faced.

Slowly, the procession pulls away, moving along a thoroughfare named for the coach: Paul Bryant Drive. Eight motorcycle patrolmen and a cruiser with its flashing rack of lights lead the way, as the vehicles behind form a long line – the hearse, the limo and the buses at the front.

It looks like a homecoming parade, The Columnist thinks. And in a way, it is.

Inside the limo, Paul Bryant Jr. gazes out the window at the mass of humanity gathered along the street. He notices that they are about to pass the stadium that also bears his father's name: Bryant-Denny Stadium. He turns to his mother, seated next to him, between him and his sister. His voice cracks when he speaks.

"That was Papa's second home. He really loved that place."

His sister is sobbing as she watches the stadium pass by.

The funeral procession makes its way toward I-59 and the point where it heads in the direction of Birmingham. Mourners line both sides of the roadway, most of them standing as if at attention. Some even snap off a respectful salute and hold it until the hearse is out of their sight. Many are crying.

As The Columnist follows in his own car in the middle of the train, he notices two dozen kindergarten students and two teachers standing beside the street, behind a chain link fence that surrounds a playground. They all hold up pink hearts cut from cardboard. On them is written, "We love you, Bear."

Inside the limo, Mary Harmon Bryant looks away from the children. She bows her head, as if in prayer, and then finally says, "Paul would adore that. Dear God, please let The Coach see those children."

Along the interstate highway, cars and trucks in both directions have pulled to the side of the road, showing their respect. Many drivers have left their vehicles and stand outside to watch the procession pass by. More than a few hold signs, red-and-white pompons or pennants. Some wear crimson jerseys or sweatshirts.

At an overpass, a dozen mourners stand reverently motionless behind a sign they have draped off the bridge. It says, "Thanks for the memories."

Later, in Birmingham, with the casket about to be lowered into the ground, Mary Harmon is led away by her children and grandchildren. Thousands of people mill about in Elmwood Cemetery, hoping to get a glimpse of the coffin before it disappears from sight. Between 5,000 and 8,000 people are there, the news media will later report.

The Columnist stands near a gathering of former players. He recognizes John David Crow, a Heisman Trophy winner when he played for Bear at Texas A&M…Joe Namath, an unlikely import to Alabama from north of the Mason-Dixon line, but a man who left Tuscaloosa considering Bear to be a second father to him…George Blanda, a Kentucky player who went on to a legendary career in the National Football League after his tutelage from Coach Bryant.

The men are quiet, as if finding the right words is impossible.

One of them finally breaks the silence.

"Can you believe this crowd?" Crow asks. "It reminds me of a football weekend in Birmingham."

It reminded The Columnist of the same thing. Legion Field was only a couple of miles away from where they stood.

"Yeah, but those games won't be the same without him on the sidelines," Namath says quietly.

"No, Joe, college football won't be the same without him," Blanda emphatically says, and there's a trace of a tear in the corner of the tough old player's eye. "Paul Bryant is the all-time champ. The greatest coach in the history of the game."

The Columnist moves away, back toward his car, already trying to compose in his head the difficult words of the story he will write that night. He must describe this day and tell of the life now suddenly ended, and why that life burned so brightly, affecting so many in such a positive way. And tell it all so it will be understood by fans and non-fans alike.

How would he ever be able to convey to anyone who had not lived in this football-loving state the stature this man held among his people? The depth of the love and admiration they had for him, far beyond any usual relationship between a football coach and the fans of his school. How he and the success of his teams had allowed people to seize their own bit of personal glory by basking in the warm glow of his aura. How he had uplifted an entire state and afforded a new source of pride to a populace that had so little else to truly be proud of in those days.

There was so much to say.

Back in the car, the announcer on the radio station is doing the same thing The Columnist has been trying to do: describe what was going on in Elmwood Cemetery that bright, winter day and what this man's life and death meant to the people who loved and respected him. He is having a tough time making the words work adequately.

But then, as The Columnist eases his automobile through the clotted traffic and makes a detour past the towering light standards and sweeping seats of Legion Field Stadium, he suddenly realizes the answer to his own questions about how to tell Bear's story.

There was only one way. That was from the beginning.

Four days after the funeral of their boss, Billy Varner is helping Linda Knowles, Bear's long-time secretary, clean out the coach's office. Memories and packed boxes are stacked all about. A nameplate and a couple of yet-empty boxes rest on a huge desk. The coach's high-back office chair is still there, as if waiting for the man to step through the door once again, sit down, light up a Chesterfield and call Pat Dye or John Forney or Bobby Bowden on the phone to quickly reconnoiter the football landscape...or maybe even talk business or fishing or golf.

Most of the walls are bare by now, though. Bare except for several framed photos, each showing players and coaches of championship football teams. The young, crew cut men are lined up proudly in uniform-number order behind massive trophies won through great personal effort and sacrifice on gridiron battlefields. Neither the bodyguard nor the secretary has seen fit to remove those photos yet.

Varner and Knowles move slowly as they carry out this unwanted task, carefully inspecting each item before relegating it to its box, as if it might hold some memory that is too dear to pack away with the rest. Both of them look drained, pale and worn down, but it isn't the hard, physical work of packing up the office that has them moving in such deliberate slow motion. Both hate to see it all come to an end. And, by shoving these mementoes into the far reaches of some dark box, it is most assuredly bringing Coach and his life here to a finality neither of them wants to contemplate just yet.

Varner finally seals up the last box then sits down on the big couch against the back wall. He reaches for a cigarette, puts it in his mouth, lights it and puffs on it for a moment.

"Linda, if it's all right with you, let's just stay in here for a little bit longer," he finally says. "I'm hurtin' too damn bad to leave right now."

Knowles eases down on the corner of the desk, a spot she has used many times when talking with her boss, taking direction, writing notes, discussing the preacher's sermon the Sunday before or the previous Saturday's game.

"I know, Billy. It's been four days since the funeral, and I'm still numb. There's too much to remember. Too much to remember."

Knowles pulls a well-used tissue from her dress pocket and wipes away tears yet again. Just when she is sure she is all cried out, there are more tears.

Billy Varner looks up at her then. There is an odd look on his face and a break in his voice when he speaks.

"Linda, it won't be anything like he said it was going to be."

Knowles glances at him quizzically but waits for him to go on, to explain his odd statement. He takes a deep draw on the cigarette and breathes out the smoke before he speaks again.

"You know what Coach Bryant always said…that he'd be forgotten as soon as we laid him to rest." Knowles nods. She heard Coach say that very thing many times. She had either paid him little mind or had pshawed such an idea. But he was always adamant about the short time that memories of him would linger once he was no longer winning football games or affecting the lives of young men and the emotions of so many other folks in the process. "Well, you can bet I heard some more of that kind of talk when we took that trip to Arkansas last month," Varner adds.

"What'd he say exactly, Billy?"

"That he knew his time was up," Varner says mournfully. "That since he wasn't walking those sidelines no more, his days were about done."

"I guess that's why he was so dead set on going back to Fordyce one more time, and why he insisted on going when he did."

"Uh huh," Billy grunts and blows another cloud of smoke into the air. "And he did some talkin' while we rode…almost like he was reviewing his whole life." He points to the piles of boxes stacked next to the big desk, the clean spots on the office wall where the championship photos have hung. "Like he was determined to explain all of these memories we just packed away."

Knowles bites her lip and asks the question she has wanted to ask for the last four days.

"Did he seem happy, Billy? On the trip, I mean?"

"Yeah, he did. He was as content as I've ever seen him." Varner exhales more smoke, watches it climb toward the ceiling of the office. A broad grin spreads over his face. It's the first time he has smiled in days. "And Linda, you should've heard the stories he told, the things he remembered. Every place we passed, it seemed to kick off some kind of memory or story he had been waitin' to tell somebody for years. Listenin' to him, it made my heart so warm I thought it'd blister!"

The old bodyguard laughs out loud then and eases back farther on the couch. He ignores the long ash on his cigarette, even when it breaks off and falls onto his shirtfront in a gray smudge. He is remembering.

Remembering the Coach's stories, just the way he spilled them out for him on that last trip home.

Home to Arkansas, where it all began.

Chapter One:

The Bear

The mule-drawn wagon meandered down a dusty dirt road, the rising sun casting the peaceful scene in dusty pink. It was only a half hour past daybreak. The day was still new, fresh and dew-washed. The wagon was loaded with fruits and vegetables, headed for the farmer's market in Fordyce, a little flatwoods town in south central Arkansas, not unlike a thousand others around the South.

Riding high on the seat, humming a familiar hymn, sat a woman wearing a simple farm dress and a bonnet on her head, clutching a rough, worn sweater close to her body to stave off the chill of the early morning. Next to her on the wagon seat was a tall, lanky boy about twelve years old, wearing overalls, a flannel shirt and work shoes. He held the reins and aggressively gee'd and haw'ed the two mules that plodded along in front of them, keeping them in the middle of the dirt roadway.

Ahead of them, the brick main street of the little town finally appeared in view around a turn in the road. They passed the sign that proclaimed the population of Fordyce to be 3,602 folks.

"It's gonna be a good day, Mama," young Paul Bryant proclaimed confidently as they

approached the town square. "I can tell because you're singing."

"Well, let's hope you're right, Paul," she replied with a smile. "We need to do good if we're to have any money this week. But about all we can be assured of is it'll be a long day, whether it's a good one or not."

"Aw, Mama, it ain't so bad." The boy pointed toward the rear ends of the mules as they pulled at the traces. "Remember old Pete and Joe got up real early this morning, too, then had to pull us and the wagon all the way to town while we rested."

Ida Bryant smiled at her son again.

"That's a fact. But I'm a far cry older than you and them two mules." She paused then added, "And probably just about as hungry, I'd guess."

Townspeople were already moving about Main Street and the couple of other byways that branched off from the square. Folks got an early start in this part of the country. There were crops to tend, animals to feed, stores to open.

"Well, then," Paul said, "Why don't I get you some cheese and crackers from Mr. Keeton's store? And maybe some cold lemonade?"

"You don't have to do that. I'll eat lunch with your Uncle John at the hotel directly. And you should, too. You know your aunt and uncle want to see how much you've grown."

Young Paul eased the mules and wagon into a vacant lot next to a livery stable just past the square. He pulled to a stop alongside about a dozen other wagons then hopped down from the seat. He ran around to the other side and helped his mother climb down to the ground before he unhitched the mules.

"Mama, I ain't dressed to eat at the hotel. Besides, I'd rather go down and wait at the train tracks until it's time to go home. Maybe I can see some of my buddies down there."

Ida clucked her tongue but told him it would be okay, to run along, but to not get into any mischief.

Young Paul Bryant worked hard. All her children did. They had to if they were to make ends meet, tugging a meager existence from their little river-bottom dirt farm. Paul had gotten up early to help her load the rest of the vegetables on the wagon, brought the mules out of the barn, hitched them up and drove the wagon all the way to town. He deserved a little playtime, she reckoned. After all, he was still only a boy, barely twelve.

Ten minutes later, Paul had found the perfect boxcar to hide in while he ate his big wedge of sharp hoop cheese and the little pack of soda crackers. The car was parked on a sidetrack, as if it was waiting for him to come along. It was empty, dark and cool inside. He loved to sit inside the cars, imagining all the exotic places far from south Arkansas where the thing had been towed. Someday, he hoped to venture beyond the river bottom and past the town square to see what the big old world looked like.

He had almost finished his lunch when he heard voices outside. Young voices. Paul recognized them at once.

He lay on his stomach and eased over next to the open door to see if he could hear what they were saying.

"I know I seen him come over here. It was that clumsy kid from over in The Bottom."

It was Clark Jordan, a twelve-year-old who lived in a house with running water and electric lights, right there in the big city of Fordyce. He and his friend, Red Latham, another city boy, were pacing back and forth alongside the boxcar. It was easy to tell these two weren't from The Bottom and that they didn't have to pull corn or slop hogs or chop cotton. Their play clothes, the ones they had on this morning, were much nicer than anything Paul ever had to wear, even to church on Sunday.

"You mean that country bumpkin Paul Bryant who claims he can run the railroad tracks all the way from Moro Creek to town in half an hour?"

Paul's face burned. He felt the anger seething inside him, but he remained still and listened to the goading tone of the two boys' voices.

"Yeah, five miles in thirty minutes. Can you imagine that?"

The two boys stopped directly beneath the boxcar door. It was clear they were talking loud enough for anyone inside the car to hear what they were saying.

"Well, he ain't nothin' but a braggin' fool," Latham said. "I'll put up two dollars against him any day."

"That boy ain't got two dollars," Jordan replied. "That's why he's hidin' inside this old boxcar. He's too ashamed to show his ugly face."

"Yep, them Bryants ain't nothin' but dirt-poor pig farmers. Everybody knows that!"

Paul gritted his teeth and fought the impulse to jump from the rail car and show those two city boys a thing or two. He tried to replay his mother's words – her admonition to not get into trouble or cause a ruckus.

He eased back into the shadows and waited, hoping the two would finally give up and go off to torture somebody else.

But their mocking words hurt like wasp stings.

"Some day," he whispered to himself. "Some day, I'll show all of you."

But then, it was simply too much. He couldn't allow these brats to talk about him and his family like that. With a horrifying, blood-curdling screech, he leapt from the boxcar door and landed, sprawling, right on top of his two tormentors.

Latham and Jordan scrambled to their feet and took off like a flash, but there was an angry Paul Bryant close behind. They stopped long enough to hurl dirt clods and rocks at him to try to slow down his bull rush, but Paul only dodged them and kept com- ing…all the way to the town square.

That night, young Paul was unusually quiet as he and his broth- ers and sisters gathered around the family table for dinner. There were so many of them and so much activity that no one noticed his somber mood. Paul was the youngest of the sons, with one younger sister.

Ida Bryant was dipping food as fast as she could, ladling up thick, fragrant chili and pouring it over cornbread in mismatched bowls set in front of each kid, trying to feed the hungry bunch as quickly as she could. Wilson Bryant sat at one end of the table, watching the process as his brood got fed, effectively keeping some semblance of order with only a raised eyebrow here and there. He was a heavy-set man, his face ruddy, as much from his perpetual high blood pressure as the heat of the sun.

Ida talked as she worked.

"It's a shame we didn't have more corn to sell this trip, Wilson. What we brought today was the talk of the town."

"If I'd of known it would turn out so good, I'd a planted another acre of it and not fooled with them pole beans the worms ate up," Wilson said. "I see you didn't have too many tomatoes left on the wagon either. Folks must've liked them, too."

Ida finally eased down into the chair at the opposite end of the table from her husband. She slumped, momentarily too tired to lift a spoon. She looked from her husband to her youngest boy as she talked.

"We might've sold the rest of 'em if your son had not pitched such a fit right there in the town square."

She settled on Paul, giving him a hard look.

"I've seen that before," Wilson said between bites of the chili.

"But this time he got into a fight with Red Latham and one of the Jordan twins."

Wilson now looked up from his chili bowl and gave the boy a hard stare of his own.

"So it was two against one, you're saying?"

"Uh huh, and young Paul thought he could even things up by throwing tomatoes."

Wilson Bryant was still staring hard at his son.

"Tell me about this fight, boy."

"There wasn't one," Paul said, his head down, staring at the uneaten food in his bowl.

"Then why did you throw tomatoes at 'em? Tomatoes we could have sold for good money?"

"They were talkin' about me...and saying bad things about us."

"Us?"

"The family. Called us dirty pig farmers and hicks."

"Mmmm. I see."

"But the worst thing was that Latham said we were losers. We may not have much, but we ain't losers, Papa."

Several of the younger siblings snickered at Paul's words, but a scathing look from Ida Bryant hushed them. She leaned toward the boy and gently pulled the long hair out of his eyes.

"I didn't know that was what started it."

Paul looked up then, at his mother and father, at his brothers and sisters. Fire flashed in his eyes.

"It don't matter, Mama. It's my war. I'll show both of them...and everybody else...that I'm a winner." He grinned then. "And maybe I'll get in their pockets at the same time."

The kids giggled again. Wilson Bryant waved his spoon at his son and looked at him through his thick eyebrows. That was his daddy's "I mean business" look. He made sure to listen when the man employed that look.

"It's one thing to have some pride, Paul. But don't go making bets you can't pay off on. It ain't right."

Paul sat up straight in his chair then, his jaw thrust forward.

"This won't be no gamble, Papa. All I'm gonna do is prove that I'm true to my word. And that I ain't nothin' but a winner."

The group of kids gathered by the railroad depot pushed and jostled at each other and kept up a continual banter, most of them already bored by the event at hand. There was a good dozen of them, two-thirds boys.

But one of them was serious about what was taking place there next to the railroad depot in Fordyce. Red Latham tried to ignore the horseplay. He held a watch and kept alternately checking it and nervously looking down the length of track where the parallel rails disappeared beyond a bank of honeysuckle a couple of hundred feet away.

"That's twenty-nine minutes and counting," Latham sang out. "And plowboy ain't nowhere in sight."

"That's twenty-eight minutes and thirty-five seconds, Red," one of the girls, Drucilla Smith, corrected him, then stuck her tongue out at him for emphasis.

"Okay, but that hick still ain't gonna make it."

"Then who's that comin' around the bend?" the girl asked with a big grin.

Sure enough, there was Paul Bryant, making the turn and lumbering up the tracks toward them. He was breathing hard and red-faced but he was still running. The legs of his overalls were pulled up above his knees and sweat stained his work shirt, but he was still moving, still jogging.

"Runners don't wear boots," Clark Jordan said disbelievingly. "Do they?"

"That one does," Drucilla noted. "He's home free if he don't fall down."

Red Latham checked his watch again, and then measured the distance Paul Bryant had yet to cover. His eyes went wide.

Paul stumbled just as he passed them and fell to the ground on his hands and knees, his chest heaving. But there was a big smile on his face as he fought for breath.

"Give me…the time…Red," he said between gasps for air.

"You had twenty ticks to spare," Drucilla sang out happily.

"Naw, he's fifteen seconds late," Latham maintained, but he hid the watch face from Drucilla and the rest.

It was Clark Jordan who set Red straight.

"Nope, that ain't right, Red. He beat us fair and square."

"So the hick got lucky!" Latham spat. "So what?"

"So fork over my two dollars," Paul Bryant said as he climbed to his feet. "And one more thing, City Boy. You better not ever let me hear you say anything bad about me or my mama or papa again, or I'll give you far worse than a tomato upside your head. You understand?"

Latham nodded grudgingly as he dug in his trouser pocket for the two silver dollars he carried there.

Drucilla Smith helped dust the gravel and dirt from Paul's overalls then cuffed him playfully on the shoulder.

"Paul, you won. That was great!"

His beet-red face grew even more crimson with Drucilla's words, but his chest swelled with pride.

She was right.

He had proved it to everyone.

Paul Bryant was nothing but a winner.

It was a hot July day in Fordyce, four years after the run up the tracks. Despite the heat and dust, the town brimmed with excitement. A traveling bear act had set up in the old theater downtown. A large crowd had gathered to watch as the bear's handler led the big animal through a few basic tricks. But then, the barker moved to the real reason he was there. He called out in a singsong voice a challenge to all the young men gathered around to come up on the stage and attempt to pin the bear to the floor.

No one seemed eager to accept the dare. The man poked the muzzled bear with a big stick, forcing the animal to stand on his back legs and growl in rage. The crowd drew back and buzzed. The creature was frightening, menacing and clearly angry enough to slap any challenger silly.

"Okay, folks, you can see that we've got a mean one here. So I'll pay a dollar a minute to anybody who can pin this critter to the ground."

The crowd oohed and aaahed, but no one stepped forward to take him up on his offer.

"Haw! Ain't there a tough man out there somewhere who'd like to impress his woman by showing her how he could tame this little old bitty teddy bear? Or are you all a bunch of chickens? Bock! Bock!"

Paul Bryant and Clark Jordan stood to one side of the stage, talking heatedly with each other while the barker continued his chanting.

"Come on, fellas. I heard you men in Arkansas was tough. Now I'm beginning to have my doubts. Maybe I ought to just get on back down to Texas and tell them folks down there that they're still the toughest, rowdiest fellers on the face of God's green earth."

Suddenly, Bryant broke toward the stage at a run, even as Jordan tried to grab his overall gallus and pull him back.

"I believe I can beat that old bear," Bryant announced to the crowd that milled about them.

"Paul, get back here," Jordan yelled after him, maintaining his hold on his friend's overalls as he tried to drag him back. "Look at them teeth. That critter can eat you alive, even as big and gawky as you are."

But Bryant pulled away again.

"Hell, Clark, that scrawny little thing has a strap around his mouth. He can't bite. This is gonna be some easy money, and I aim to win it."

Up on the stage, the bear handler had noticed the tussle to his left. He was still needling the crowd, trying to work it into enough of a frenzy that one of the fools would climb up on the stage and give it a try.

"Then it's one, two, three, four and out the door. A real Texan like myself can't waste time with a bunch of Arkansas cowards."

But just then, Paul Bryant broke through the crowd, ran toward the stage and hopped up onto the edge. He ignored Clark Jordan's shouted warning.

"Paul, this ain't like running the railroad track. That grizzly bear is gonna gnaw you into little old pieces and spit you out."

Too late. Bryant was already facing the bear, standing but four feet away from the growling creature. He was concentrating on the animal's big paws and flashing teeth inside the muzzle and didn't notice that his sister, Kathryn, three years older and far wiser, had joined the crowd in the theater. She couldn't believe that was her baby brother up there on that stage staring down a mad grizzly bear.

"Paul William Bryant! You get down from there before you get killed!" she yelped. "And if you do get killed, you know Mama will use a switch on you!"

He didn't even look her way when he yelled to her, "Sit down and watch, Kathryn. I'm about to make us rich."

The handler grinned. The fun was about to begin. He poked the bear again hard with his stick.

Bryant still faced the animal, bent over in a half crouch like a standup wrestler. But the critter apparently didn't care for the subtleties of wrestling. It dropped to all fours and made a sudden, fearsome lunge toward its latest human challenger.

Paul adroitly stepped aside to avoid the takedown move but he couldn't avoid the sudden swipe of the bear's paw as it lumbered past. Its claws opened an ugly cut on Bryant's neck just beneath his right ear. He felt the sting and put his hand to the cut, then studied the blood on his palm for a moment.

"Somebody stop this!" Kathryn Bryant hollered to no one in particular. "That thing's cutting my brother to pieces!"

On stage, though, Paul was back in wrestling form, moving about in a slow circle, keeping his distance from the mad bear while he considered what the animal's next move might be. Then, after sucking in a deep breath of the hot air, he abruptly leapt at the animal, grabbed it by its shaggy hair and neck muscles, and with a mighty grunt, threw the big beast to the floor with an awful crunch. The bear used what air was left in its lungs to growl in anger and frustration, but the thing couldn't seem to break Paul's tight hold.

The bear was pinned and couldn't get loose.

Clark Jordan was standing next to the stage, hopping up and down excitedly, but now shouting encouragement to his friend.

"Hold what you got, buddy. The seconds are passing and the money box is gettin' fuller and fuller."

Bryant had the bear in a powerful hug, one the varmint couldn't get out of. Meanwhile, the handler had sized up the situation. For the first time, he might actually have to pay off his challenge. That wasn't part of the program. He began kicking Paul in the ribs, poking him with his stick instead of the bear, trying to get him to let loose of his animal.

"Leave him alone, mister. He's whipping the hell out of your old bear!" Jordan yelled. The crowd joined in, chanting, "Go, Paul, go! Go, Paul, go!"

The man took note of the townspeople's disposition. There was sure more of them than there was of him, and his bear didn't seem to be in any position to help. He stepped back and pled with his bear to get loose. But the animal was stuck.

The handler didn't see the muzzle slipping off the bear's mouth. Bryant didn't notice either. He grinned at the crowd as he used his weight and muscle to keep the animal pinned, trying to calculate how much time had passed, how much money he was making.

"The strap, Paul! The damn strap is coming off its mouth!" Jordan warned.

"Oh, God in heaven, my brother is about to be dead," Kathryn wailed.

Without losing his grip, Paul moved his body enough so that he could see the bear's frothing mouth. Sure enough, the strap that kept the critter from being able to bite had just about worked its way loose and the bear was tugging at it with his tongue, trying to get it off.

Behind him, the bear's handler watched wide-eyed. He had a pretty good idea what his animal could do if it got free and could bite and tear at its tormentor.

"Save yourself, boy!" Jordan called. "Let that thing go and take a leap!"

Bryant quickly obliged. He rolled off the top of the bear and jumped to his feet, all in one motion, then took a running leap off the stage and landed in the front row of seats, cutting both shins badly. The bear's handler had managed to get a rope around the enraged animal's neck and was tugging with all his might to get it out an exit at the back of the stage. The animal pulled the other way, trying to get off the stage and to where Paul Bryant lay sprawled among the spectators.

From where he had landed in the crowd, Paul could see the bear and its handler trying to get away. He still wasn't afraid of the grizzly, and he ignored the pain in his legs. His only thought was of the money he was owed. He had won, and he meant to collect.

He let some of the crowd help him to his feet and took off after the two, just as they disappeared through an opening at the back of the stage.

Behind him, a dancing Clark Jordan was waving his arms, leading the crowd in a jubilant, hypnotic cheer.

"Bear Bryant! Bear Bryant! Bear Bryant!" they chanted, their words echoing throughout the old theater like a pep rally in a gym filled with loud, boisterous fans.

"Bear Bryant!"

Chapter Two:

Cleats

The football was planted firmly on the opponents' two-yard line. Though time was running out, nobody appeared to be in any significant hurry. The Fordyce Redbug team was safely ahead, the game well in hand. The players on the field stood huddled together in their rough, worn uniforms, sweat-stained and even a bit bloody from the battle they had fought for the past two hours. Several of the Redbugs had removed their leather helmets during the timeout, awaiting word from the sidelines on whether or not to simply take a knee and let the game end or go ahead and score on their opponents one more time.

The home crowd that filled the rough bleachers on one side of the field had voted already. They wanted blood. It had been a while since a Redbug team had had such a year as this, and they wanted to savor every victory. They knew their team was on its way to the 1930 Arkansas state high school championship, but every touchdown was precious.

Just then, a tall, muscular player trotted from the sidelines out to the huddle. He stooped down, hands on his knees, as they began to once again strap on their helmets and get ready for the play the coach had sent in.

"Okay, here's what we're going to do," Click Jordan, the tailback, told them. "We're going to snap the ball from center to ol' Bear and let him run it in for the score."

"Like hell," the center protested. "He ain't scoring any touchdowns as long as I'm doing the centering."

But Click told him to shut up and center the ball.

The referee was blowing his whistle, motioning them to break the huddle and get the game over with.

"If you score a touchdown, you'll be the first one to ever do it without the football," the center growled.

But Paul Bryant ignored him. He tapped him on the shoulder pad.

"Just center me the ball, Ike. Then block. I'll head for right end."

"You ain't nothin' but a ham, Bear," the other player spat. "And you're not gonna score no touchdown."

The rest of the players hustled up to the line, ignoring the sad looks on the faces of their opponents. The other team was beaten, and they showed it.

Bear took a position directly behind the center, five yards back, while the quarterback lined up behind the tackle on the right side of the line, as if he was getting ready to block for his teammate.

"Down! Ready!" Bryant barked in his already-deep voice. "Hut one! Hut two!"

On "Two!" the center snapped the ball hard and straight but a good six feet over Bryant's head. It shot backward, finally hit the ground and rolled crookedly down the field, with Bear in pursuit, trying to corral the thing before the other team could get to it. When he finally scooped it up, it seemed the entire defensive squad was bearing down on him. They appeared to be suddenly rejuvenated, ready to take revenge on this one play for the beating Bryant and his teammates had inflicted on them all night.

Just before they swarmed all over him, Bryant caught a glimpse of the rest of the Redbug team standing there, either watching or rolling around on the grass in obvious glee.

There was no place to go. Bryant dived for the dirt and was immediately covered by the entire opposition. Then, through the mass of humanity on top of him, he heard the laughter and jibes from his teammates.

"Bear, you still want the ball?" the center sang.

From underneath that pile of bodies, even Paul cracked a smile.

Paul Bryant made a strange sight. There he was, a tall, lanky 17-year old, standing barefoot in the door of the shoe repair shop just off the square. He held his work boots in his hand, waiting for a lady to complete her business with the shop's proprietor. He breathed in the smell of leather and shoe polish and liniment and waited patiently for the lady to finish up.

"Thank you, Mr. Clark," she was saying. "As usual, you did a wonderful job."

"I appreciate that, Mrs. Cox. Please come back to see us."

The woman ran right into Paul as she turned to leave.

"Excuse me, ma'am," he said politely and stepped aside to let her through.

"Well, well, if it ain't 'Bear' Bryant," Mr. Clark said with a chuckle. "The meanest feller between Fordyce and Texarkana."

"Yes, sir," Bryant said, clearly embarrassed. "Mr. Clark, I was..."

"Tell me, son. Is it true that they never did track down that scalawag that took off without paying you what you won when you whipped that old bear?"

"Yes, sir, but right now, I'm more interested..."

"Well, they oughta find him yet and put the cuffs on him and put him under the jail! I was there, and I know what a dang brave thing it was that you did."

"Thank you, Mr. Clark," Bryant said. He held up his scuffed, worn work boots. "Pardon me, sir, but I was wondering what you'd charge to put me some new spikes on these boots?"

Clark looked surprised.

"Spikes, huh? You must've worn the old ones down to the nub when the Redbugs won the state championship. Can y'all do it again this year?"

"Yes, sir. But there's no way I can stand up on that clay field without new cleats."

Clark took one of the boots and looked it over.

"I hope you got another pair for school and church."

Bryant dropped his head and blushed. Slowly, painfully, he shook it.

"No, sir."

"I see. Well, I can handle the job all right."

"Mr. Clark, I need a good pair of spikes. This is my last chance to show what I can do...my best shot at ever getting a football scholarship to go to college. Like Don Hutson and those other slicks from Pine Bluff."

Clark frowned.

"Yeah, but that traitor went to Alabama."

Bryant didn't hesitate.

"Yes, sir, he did. But he's gonna get to play in the Rose Bowl for the Crimson Tide someday...and I hope I'm on the field with him."

Clark shook his head but grinned at his tall, muscular young customer.

"All right, Bear. Give me that other boot and let me get to work on 'em."

"And Mr. Clark, that ain't all," the young man went on, his voice rising with excitement. "I got other plans. When I'm finished playing at Alabama, I figure on being a coach like Knute Rockne or Pop Warner." He handed the cobbler his other boot and stood with his hands on his hips. "When that happens, I'll own a farm instead of having to work on one all the time."

Clark shook his head.

"Boy, do you know how different it is playing college ball than running around out there for the Redbugs?"

"The object of the game is still the same, Mr. Clark. All you have to do is chase down the guy that's totin' the football and knock him on his butt. Kinda like I did that old bear."

The old cobbler laughed out loud.

"You know, Bear, you might just live out that dream after all. You just might!"

Chapter Three:

Remember the Rose Bowl

The family that was gathered around the supper table was smaller than before. Some of the Bryant children had left home already and gone out to make their own way. And the setting was different, too. They were no longer in the rough farmhouse down in The Bottom, where the kids had done most of their growing up.

Ida and Wilson Bryant now ran a boarding house in Fordyce. Though still not rich by any means, it was obvious that the family was doing better. Some of the children that pulled up to the table were still barefoot on this hot August evening, but their clothes were store-bought, not stitched together from feed sacks.

Once all the food was on the table, Ida Bryant eased down in her chair next to where her husband sat at the end.

"Papa, I want you to offer a nice prayer tonight," she said. "A special one that'll help Paul once he gets down to Alabama."

Bear Bryant was eighteen years old and about to go away to college on a full football scholarship, even though he would have to

finish up his high school degree once he got to Tuscaloosa. Coach Hank Crisp, an assistant coach from Alabama, had come to town, trying to recruit the Jordan twins from the Redbug team. Bryant had been only too ready to agree to go to Tuscaloosa with them to play for the legendary coach. He was chomping at the bit, rearing to get on down to the home of the Rose Bowl champions.

And he didn't think he needed any special prayers said on his behalf.

"Aw, Mama, come on," he growled. "It ain't like I'm still wet behind the ears and ain't never been any farther away from here than Pine Bluff."

"I know that, son, but our flock keeps gettin' smaller and smaller. You're our baby boy, and now, here you are going off…"

Wilson Bryant interrupted her, his head bowed, with the beginning of his blessing.

"Dear Lord, we thank you for this food and trust it will be used for the nourishment of our bodies. Oh, and that we'll all be safe until we're together again, and that Paul will win all the games he plays in. Amen."

Paul raised his head with the others.

"My gosh, Papa, it's not like I'm going off to war or anything. And I don't reckon God has much of a care who wins or loses in a game of football."

Wilson reached for the big bowl of whipped potatoes and began slapping them onto his plate.

"Maybe that's right. But from what all they're saying about Coach Frank Thomas, you better be ready to play football like you're fightin' a war."

Ida had a worried scowl on her face.

"I still don't see why you can't go up to Arkansas. Coach Thomsen was so nice and all. And he even took you boys way off down to Dallas to watch that all-star game with him last year."

"It's a wonder he let me ride back home with him. You know he caught me sneaking off and trying to find a radio, just so I could listen to Alabama beat Washington State in the Rose Bowl."

"Well, then, you better listen to Coach Thomas," his mother said. "Maybe he'll make you stronger."

"And a whole lot tougher," his father added through a mouthful of green beans.

"Well, think about it, Papa," Bryant said, sitting back in his chair. "There's not much in life any tougher than plowing a mule all day long. And the rewards a man can get from football are a far cry better than what he could ever get from farming that river bottom land."

Wilson Bryant looked up from his plate, his loaded fork paused in mid-air.

"Now I can agree with that, son. I can most certainly agree with that."

The rowdy locker room finally quieted when it came time for the coach to speak. Frank Thomas didn't look much like a football coach at all, but more like a short, pudgy English professor or an insurance salesman. Still, when he spoke, everyone listened. It was November, 1934, in the home team dressing room at Birmingham's Legion Field. The team bore all the signs of battle: sweat, blood and mud. But it was clear from their demeanor that they had won another football game on this chilly, gray afternoon.

As the room stilled, the strains of the marching band outside spilled into the room. They were playing a familiar melody, "California, Here I Come."

"Men, if I don't miss my bet, that band is playing a most appropriate song," the coach shouted. The players and everyone else in the locker room cheered until Thomas motioned for them to be quiet again. "And that's because you answered every challenge...every test...all season long. Gentlemen, it's my opinion that you are most deserving of a trip to Pasadena!"

Again the players cheered, slapped each other on the backs, did their own little impromptu dances around the crowded, steamy dressing room. Coach Thomas yelled to be heard above the din.

"So where are we going?"

"California!" came the answering scream.

"For what?" the coach asked and held his hand to his ear as if to better hear their answer. One of those yelling the loudest was a tall, beefy end named Paul Bryant.

"The Rose Bowl!"

This time Thomas allowed the noise to die out on its own before he spoke again.

"Well, it's good to be happy. That's what winning is all about, and you boys are all winners. But listen to me. You clowns will have to get serious real quick. You'll have to give it everything you got to beat Stanford."

There was a chorus of disbelief. This team would have no trouble beating a team like Stanford.

"Hey, boys, it's a serious game out there. They're a fine football team. I don't want any funny stuff. We'll need to concentrate if we have any hope of beating those guys. Have I made myself clear?"

"Yes, sir!" they all sang in unison.

"Are you sure?"

"Yes, sir!" they repeated, loud enough surely to be heard all the way to the West Coast.

"All right, then. Let's go out to California and make all Alabamians proud."

Each roll of the dice elicited a refrain, a chorus made up equally of cheers and groans. The burly young men had pulled back the hotel room's furniture, stacked it against the walls and were using the thick carpet for a vigorous game of craps.

"Fall soft, ivory, fall soft," one of them pleaded. He blew on the dice in his hands and gave them a toss across the fancy rug.

"Seven come, seven go!" another shouted.

But just then, Paul Bryant burst through the hotel room door, a stricken look on his face.

"Somebody has to help me!" he said.

"Damn, Bryant, can't you see we have a game going on over here?" one of the players asked.

"Man, you look like you ran into King Kong out yonder on Sunset Strip," another added.

"Oh, it's worse than that," Bryant said as he fell hard into one of the plush chairs. "I need help bad. Mary Harmon and Barbara Dell Simmons are both downstairs in the lobby, and they're sure to start comparing notes on who invited both of them to come out here."

The dice game was now temporarily forgotten. Everyone moved to where Bryant sat, wringing his hands.

"Well, Bryant, what did you expect when you asked both of them to come watch you play?"

A pale Paul Bryant looked up at his teammates.

"I invited Mary Harmon when I heard that Barbara Dell wouldn't be able to make it. Now, I got both of 'em out here and there's just one of me!"

The room erupted into riotous laughter.

"Bryant, you may not be the dumbest man on planet Earth, but you got to be in the top ten. Here we are, three days away from playing for the national championship, and you're out here building triangles."

Bear was thinking this whole episode might be even worse than the night Coach Crisp caught him and a bunch of his teammates coming in after curfew from the Chi Omega sorority house. That escapade led to each of them running a brutal one hundred laps, right there in front of most of the student body during an important track meet. No telling what the outcome might be if those two girls ran into each other and starting discussing the purpose of their trips to the west coast.

"I was playing Barbara Dell for something else," Bryant said. "I didn't have any idea she would actually show up out here. Boys, my goose is cooked."

One of his buddies eased down into the chair next to him.

"Look, didn't you tell me that you love Mary Harmon? That you intend to marry her someday?" Bryant nodded forlornly. "Then you better tell her that…and see if you can stay clear of Barbara Dell so she don't scalp you with a dull hatchet."

Paul Bryant could only sink lower in the chair and rub his temples and contemplate how he had ever gotten himself into this mess.

The noise of the crowd was so overwhelming that the two radio commentators could hardly hear each other. They shouted into their microphones.

"Well, Bud, I suppose it is true what they say about this Crimson Tide team, the pride of Dixie. I'm not sure the Rose Bowl has ever seen such a powerful squad as this one."

"Absolutely right. This has been a Howell-to-Hutson, Howell-to-Bryant show to remember. Today, this Alabama team is the pride of the nation."

Down on the field, the Alabama defensive players were kneeling, taking their stances as the Stanford team stepped once again to the line of scrimmage, trying to salvage something from the beating they were taking. Paul Bryant was set, ready, but he suddenly spied something to his right, something apparently more important than the Stanford offensive line. He abruptly shuffled over to whatever it was that he had spotted. It was several coins dropped there by someone during the halftime show. He gathered them into his fist and hurriedly shuffled sideways, back to his position, to get ready for the beginning of the next play.

The quarterback barked his signals, and the ball was snapped, sending both teams into frenzied motion. Still clinging to his coins, Bryant sprang forward from his stance, popped the offensive lineman so hard with a shoulder and a shattering forearm that the bigger man seemed to wilt away, toppling to the ground like a fallen tree. And then he met the running back almost at the same instant that the player was handed the football. The impact was so vicious the coins flew from Bear's hand, but the runner was on his back on the Rose Bowl turf, a look of pain on his face and no air left in his lungs.

But Paul Bryant wasn't paying any attention to the health of the man he had just tackled. He was on all fours, scrambling around once again, trying to retrieve the money he had dropped in the collision.

"What in hell are you doin', son?" one of the other defenders asked.

"I'm trying to reap some of the real spoils of victory," Bryant said with a broad grin.

After the game, Coach Frank Thomas was standing before the nation's media. He couldn't help goading them a bit.

"Gentlemen, in summary, please allow me to note that all of you underestimated this fine group of young men from Alabama."

"Coach, the one we couldn't get a handle on was your other end...the one opposite Hutson. What was his name again?"

Frank Thomas fairly beamed when he answered.

"Sir, that kid's name is Bryant. B...R...Y...A...N...T. And while I may have had more talented players on my club before, I've never had one with such an interest in the game of football. Nor one with a greater desire to be a winner. Gentlemen, it is my wager that this other end of mine is tough enough mentally and physically – and has natural desire enough – to become a great coach at a very early age once his career as a player here at Alabama is completed next year. You gentlemen better get used to the name of Paul Bryant."

Coach Thomas gazed for a while at the player who was seated in the chair across from him. The young man's crutches were leaning against the chair. His leg was wrapped tightly in a bandage.

"Paul, I don't have to remind you of where we're playing this week, do I?"

"No, sir. Tennessee. In Knoxville."

The coach pinched his chin thoughtfully for a moment and studied the ceiling of his office.

"Yes. The old bitter rival. General Neyland and his troops."

"Yes, sir. I know what a big game it is."

"And this year, we have to go up there without Howell and Hutson...the type leaders who realize what it means to our team and fans to beat Tennessee. They knew we were talking war when it came to this game on our schedule every year."

"I know, Coach, and we can handle it this year," Bryant said. But Thomas' eyes were far away now, as if he was reliving some old battle he had fought long ago.

He suddenly jerked back to the present and motioned toward his player's bandaged limb.

"How's your leg by now?"

"It's broken in the shin."

"Hell, Bryant, I know that. What I'm wondering is how it feels."

"Well, Coach Tommy, the thing hurts."

Thomas was rubbing his chin again, as if studying his senior end's answer in depth. He leaned forward when he spoke again.

"But you're tough, son. You've been through a lot, here and in life. You lost your father. You've worked hard to have the kind of season we're having. You're a star on a pretty good football team."

"Yes, sir."

"Well, Bryant, tell you what. I'm going to take you with us up to Knoxville this week…just in case that leg of yours gets to feeling better once you get there and get a glimpse of those orange jerseys."

That night, Paul sat with the former Mary Harmon Black in the swing on the front porch of her sorority house. It was a pleasant autumn evening, the air still warm but the leaves already turning brilliant colors. Some of them were even Tennessee orange.

Mary Harmon rested her head on Paul's shoulder as they rocked quietly, not talking much, just enjoying being with each other. Though she was from a wealthy family, a beauty queen and had moved in high social circles, she had fallen in love at once with this rough farmer's son from Arkansas. And, their different backgrounds aside, they made a truly handsome couple.

They were clearly in love…in love and secretly married. The two had slipped off to Ozark, in south Alabama, the previous June and tied the knot. He had not told his coach for fear of losing his football scholarship. Coach Thomas did not approve of his players marrying.

Mary Harmon finally lifted her head from his shoulder and looked up at Paul.

"I'm not sure I like all the attention I'm getting, being with a big football star like you, Paul," she said. "Especially with everybody talking about you and your broken leg." She nodded toward his crutches, propped against the wall nearby.

"I guess that means you're jealous," he teased.

"No, it means I'll have to stay seated through the entire homecoming dance," she said with a slight smile.

He looked down at her and smiled back.

"Well, the doctor says it should be completely healed in three weeks." He winked at her. "But I might be able to waltz pretty good in two."

Mary Harmon laughed softly.

"You see that you are able to do that then, big boy."

Paul shifted slightly in the swing.

"But what I won't be able to do is listen to the game Saturday with you like we had planned to do."

"And just why not?"

"'Cause I'm going to Knoxville with the team."

"But Paul William Bryant, you can't even walk, much less play football."

"Hell, Mary Harmon, I know that. But Coach Tommy has come up with some kind of gimmick that might make me well quicker."

She looked at him through squinted, doubting eyes.

"What kind of gimmick?"

"I don't know what it is. He just said he would be putting me on the 'itinerary.' I figured that must be some kind of miracle healing machine."

Mary Harmon Bryant shook her head, and both of them laughed out loud.

The air in the locker room was electric. The rumble of the Tennessee faithful outside was constant, but the Alabama team was, to a man, firm-jawed and ready. Assistant Coach Hank Crisp stood in the middle of them now, ready to give one of his patented speeches. He was a fiery man, his eyes blazing, his chin thrust out as he punched the air for emphasis with his one good hand.

"Gentlemen, I know what it's like to play the Volunteers up here. That's why Coach Tommy asked me to say a few words to you before you go out on that field of battle to uphold the honor of your school and your state." Crisp paused and made eye contact with as many of his troops as he could manage in a sweep of the room. "Now I know you veterans are going to get after them. You seniors…this is your last chance to beat this bunch. And I know that includes old number 34. I don't have any doubts about him. He'll be in there scrappin' and fightin' until there ain't a drop of blood left in his body!" The coach looked each of them in the eye again, the steeliness in his own eyes a sure sign of how certain he was of what he was saying to them. Then, when he resumed his speech, his voice grew louder and louder with each word. "Old number 34! That man is courageous! That man is tough! That man has what it takes! Old number 34 is what Alabama football is all about! Ain't that right, number 34?"

Paul Bryant cheered right along with the rest of them, looked at Coach Crisp looking at him and glanced down at the number on his jersey. Number 34! His eyes grew wide. Jersey numbers often changed from week to week so the school could sell copies of the program before each game. Bryant had completely forgotten that he wore number 34 this week.

Without hesitation, he jumped to his feet, ignoring the sharp shaft of pain that shot up his broken shinbone.

"That's right, Coach Hank!" He grabbed the crutches out of the locker behind him and threw them down on the cement floor. "I'm gonna go out there and play me some football. There isn't an

Alabama man who'd let a little broken bone stop him from getting after Tennessee!"

With that, Bear Bryant, without even a sign of a limp, led the rest of the cheering squad out the dressing room door and toward the battlefield.

Three hours later, Bryant and a trainer walked slowly, happily back toward the dressing room. Now, Bear was limping slightly, but there was a broad smile on his handsome face anyway. The few Alabama fans who had managed to get tickets to the game were still in the nearly empty stands, still hoarsely chanting, "Roll Tide! Roll Tide!" over and over again.

"Just another day at the office, huh?" the trainer asked him.

"Well, I'd call it a bone-crushing win," Bryant said with a wink.

A reporter ran to catch up with them, looked hard at Bryant's bandaged leg and then said with a scowl, "Bryant, I'm from the Atlanta paper. I demand to see an x-ray of your so-called bad leg before you try to pull this same stunt against Georgia next week." The reporter looked at Bryant sideways. "If that leg's broke, I'm a danged old moo-cow."

It was the trainer who responded.

"Well, hold still while I get a bucket. We could use us a drink of victory milk right about now!"

Chapter Four:

Dream Deal

Fortunately, there was little traffic on the narrow two-lane highway, so he was making good time through the flat delta land in eastern Arkansas and through west Tennessee, headed back toward Nashville. The radio station he had been listening to faded out with the miles, so he twisted the dial to try to tune in something else. He was shocked to hear his name spoken on the radio.

"Bryant is a former Alabama star and has been an assistant coach for the past six years at both his alma mater and at Vanderbilt."

He turned the volume up louder.

"Again, we have learned that Paul 'Bear' Bryant will be named the new head football coach at Arkansas within the week. We have confirmed that Bryant was in Fayetteville to interview for the job, and it almost certainly will be his."

Paul Bryant happily tapped the steering wheel in time with the music that came on the radio after the announcer had told the world about his new job. He grinned.

The trees were almost totally bare. It was a gray early-December day, but Bryant's emotions soared. How great would it be to come back to his home state to coach the Razorbacks in his first head coaching position?

The music on the radio stopped abruptly, but Bear was only half listening. That is, until he noticed the tone in the announcer's voice.

"Folks, I don't know how this can be possible. The Associated Press is reporting that Japan has bombed the U.S. Naval base at Pearl Harbor, Hawaii. Many servicemen have been killed. Meanwhile, there are reports out of Washington that it is only a matter of hours before our nation declares war against Japan."

Bryant eased the car to the side of the road. He sat there for a moment, miles from anywhere, pondering the situation, and then pounded the steering wheel with the heel of his big hand.

He drove on, stopping in the next town, looking for a pay phone. He found one in the tiny train station. Everyone around him was chattering about the bombing of Pearl Harbor. It was real. He had not dreamed the whole thing.

It was good to hear Mary Harmon's voice on the other end of the phone line. She had heard the news, too.

"Well, it looks like I'll be fighting instead of coaching," he told her. "I guess Coach Tommy was right when he used to say that timing was everything."

"Do you think the people at Arkansas will hold the job open for you? For a while anyway?"

"There's no way, baby. Besides, this thing could last for a while."

"But you still might not get drafted."

He swallowed hard.

"That doesn't matter, honey. We're going to war. That means I'm headed for the Navy."

He could almost see her smile as she told him, "Well, okay then. But your daughter is going to have a fit without her favorite daddy around."

"You just tell Mae Martin that her old man is off making those damned Japs pay because they screwed up his dream deal."

"Don't worry, Paul. If this isn't meant to be, it will happen some-where else. You're destined to coach football...to be a head coach. Everybody knows that. You'll get your chance when this is all over."

He closed his eyes tight and tried to smile. He could only pray she was right.

It was a warm July afternoon in Chicago. The two men chatting with each other on the sidelines at the college all-star game practice seemed, at first glance, to be an odd pair. One was decked out in Navy dress whites. The other wore a business suit. Still, despite their outward differences, they seemed to be speaking a common lan-guage.

"So tell me, Paul, does the Maryland job hold any interest for you?"

The questioner was Preston Marshall, the 45-year-old owner of the Washington Redskins National Football League team.

"Well, I guess it would be a way to get back into coaching. I know I've been away for a few years, except for coaching the pre-flight squad down in North Carolina, but I was hoping it wouldn't make any difference. I just really wasn't interested in being an assis-tant coach anymore because I'm 32 years old now and..."

"Hold on, Paul. I didn't say anything about being an assistant."

Paul Bryant looked the older man in the eye.

"What are you saying then?"

"That you can be the head coach at the University of Maryland, provided you can get out of that uniform in time for the start of the season."

Only a few days later, Bear Bryant was spending his last few days aboard a Navy vessel, docked in port. He was on deck talking to a group of sailors, each burly and clearly athletic.

"You're not kidding about this?" one of them asked, the doubt obvious in his voice.

"Absolutely not," Bryant said. "Preston Marshall helped me get the job. Next week, as soon as I get my separation papers from the Navy, I'm going to get a chance to meet my team."

"That's too much luck," another of the sailors said.

"Luck ain't got nothing to do with it," Bryant said emphatically. "It's timing. And for once, it's working out for me. But the truth is I have to field a competitive team in two weeks. And frankly, I'm scared to think about the kind of players I'm about to inherit. Come to think about it, I might be better off staying in Uncle Sam's Navy. At least I know I'll get to eat tomorrow."

One of the sailors, a tall, lanky man, leaned over the railing, spit into the water below and then turned back to Bryant.

"So let me get this straight. You're recruiting us to go play for the Maryland Terps."

"Now you got the picture," Bryant said. "And it ain't a bad deal at all. You get to play football against college boys. And all the time you're whipping some ass out there on the field, you'll be getting a free education, too."

Another sailor clipped the tall man on the shoulder.

"And we know we can do it. We're good. We're service champs."

"Now you're talking," Bear assured him. "What's more, I've got a dozen other military veterans just like you guys ready to put on the uniform for Maryland."

"Then I'm with you, Bear!"

"Me, too," another chimed in.

"Great," the young coach said. "But there's one thing."

"What's that?"

"From right now forward, I'm not 'Bear.' I'm 'Coach Bryant' to all of you. You can still call me 'Bear' when we're drinking whiskey, celebrating victories. But on that field, practice or game, I'm 'Coach Bryant.'"

The men all nodded. The idea was clearly growing on them. But one sailor in the bunch had a doubtful look on his face.

"But Bear...Coach Bryant. That's been a losing program for several seasons now. Sounds to me like they've learned to lose real good."

Bryant looked at him hard but then winked and smiled.

"Yeah, that's right. It has been a bad deal for them lately. But that's about to change in a big hurry. With the fine coach they've hired and the hard butts that coach is recruiting to play football at Maryland, College Park is about to be one of the happiest places on the planet come Saturday afternoons."

With that, Bear turned and walked away. The tall, lanky sailor watched him go then slapped a couple of his shipmates on their backs.

"One thing about old Bear...I mean Coach Bryant. He's as cocky as he is good. I just hope the Terps appreciate what they're about to be getting."

The atmosphere in the president's office was icy and thick, the tension palpable. Curly Byrd, the president of the University of Maryland, sat fuming behind his big desk. Across from him, Paul "Bear" Bryant stood defiantly, stretched to his full height. The president studied the letter of resignation the coach had put before him. The longer he considered it, the madder he got.

"Damn you, Bryant!" he finally sputtered. "I give you the break of a lifetime – a chance to coach at one of the finest schools in the country – and you walk away from Maryland after only one season. That's the most ungrateful thing I've ever heard of!" He seemed on the verge of exploding. He stood suddenly and tried to pull himself up to the same level as his stubborn head football coach. "I'm not going to let you do it. I'm not letting you resign."

Bryant's voice was firm and solid when he answered his boss.

"You know that I'm leaving with damn good reason."

"I ought to haul you into court."

"With all due respect, President Byrd, but you're impossible. You would think a 6-2-1 record in our first year would be enough to keep your nose out of my affairs. Have you forgotten that this program had one win season before last? One win!"

Byrd's face was still crimson with anger.

"Don't you forget that I coached for twenty-three years myself. And that I know something about this game."

Paul Bryant didn't hesitate.

"But you don't know a damn thing about dealing with people."

Byrd was still so angry he could hardly make the words spill out without them getting all jumbled up.

"Just don't you forget that I run this school. Nobody else. Me."

"And don't you forget, President Byrd, that I was hired to run this football program. And that's why you don't fire my assistant coaches. And you don't decide that a lazy-ass tackle gets another chance on my team. I got rid of that fat slob for good reason. Then you let him come back because you're scared of his rich daddy. That's not how winners do things. Not by a long shot!"

Byrd slammed his fist down onto the desk. Figurines on the desk rattled in reaction to the force of the blow.

"I'm not going to let a cocky, non-combat veteran, who just got lucky with some influential friends, talk to me like that."

Bryant shrugged.

"Fine. I'm gone. I have no intention of staying anywhere where I can't run my own program the way I think it needs to be run."

Byrd shook his head.

"You're an idiot, Bryant. You're a young, hotheaded coach with no place else to go. You'll be lucky if you ever coach above the high school level again."

When he got back to his office, Paul Bryant slammed his door shut behind him with enough force to make the pictures on the wall dance. He didn't know who to be maddest at, Curly Byrd or himself.

Byrd might be right. There might not be anywhere else to go once word got out about how this situation had played out.

He had just quit his first head-coaching job after only one season. He had no prospects for another position. And to top it off, his office was a mess. He had been out recruiting for Maryland and had not had a chance to deal with the piles of mail and paperwork that had been accumulating. His first inclination was to sweep the whole mess into a file drawer somewhere and let his successor deal with it all.

But, for some reason, a yellow telegram envelope on top of the stack caught his eye. He used an index finger to rip it open. As he read the message inside, his eyes grew big in disbelief.

Timing! Again, it was timing! Coach Tommy had been dead right.

"Bear: If you are interested in becoming the head coach at the University of Kentucky, call me as soon as possible." And the note was signed by Dr. Herman Donovan, the president of the school.

Paul Bryant was already humming the tune to "My Old Kentucky Home" as he picked up the phone to call Mary Harmon and tell her the news.

The next morning at breakfast, Mary Harmon and Paul were talking about the headline in the morning paper. The story was on the front page. It was that big a news story that the University of Maryland's young coach was departing after only one season. Their daughter, Mae Martin, was nine, and she listened as her parents talked. She was old enough to know this meant another move for the family. Paul Junior, only one year old, sat in his stroller nearby, showing little interest in the breakfast-table discussion.

"How did that reporter find out so fast that we were leaving?" Mary Harmon asked.

"They probably heard me and the president hollering at each other."

"Were you mad, Daddy?" Mae Martin asked.

Bear chuckled.

"Yeah, you might say that."

Mary Harmon finished reading the story and dropped the paper among the dirty dishes on the table.

"At least there's no mention of the Kentucky job. That'd be the wrong…"

The phone pealed in the next room. Husband and wife looked at each other for a moment. Mary Harmon went to answer it. The voice on the other end of the line was calm and conciliatory.

"Mary Harmon, it's Curly Byrd. Is Bear still there?"

"Yes, sir. Just a moment."

Bear cleared his throat before he said, "Yes, sir?"

"Bear, I've got a problem, and you are the only one that can help me. The students are skipping class today because you're leaving."

"That's stupid of them to do."

"That's for damn sure. But I need you to meet me in front of the student union and talk to them…like at 10 o'clock."

Bryant looked at his watch, thought for a moment, smiled and said, "I'll be there at 11."

It was an ugly scene in front of the union building. A sizeable crowd of students milled about, shouting, some carrying signs saying, "Keep the Coach, Fire the President" and "We Want Bear, Not Byrd."

The crowd grew quiet when they saw Bear Bryant stand before them to speak.

"Listen, I just want you folks to know that you need to go on back to class. It's not that I don't love the University of Maryland and its football program. I just got an offer that I can't refuse. The president has assured me that all this will be forgotten if you go on back to class peacefully."

Most of the angry students began wandering away.

Curly Byrd shook Bryant's hand.

"Bear, I really appreciate that."

"Right. But you need to know I only did this for one reason. I don't want the president at Kentucky to think I'm some kind of troublemaker."

With that, Bear Bryant turned his back and walked away, leaving behind his first head-coaching job. Somebody else out there had called for him, somebody who promised him that he could do whatever it took to make this new team a winner.

That was all Bear Bryant needed to hear.

Chapter Five:

Wrath of the Baron

It was good to be wanted. Good to see the loud and happy group of students gathered in the auditorium in Lexington. Good to see the signs that read, "The Blue Grass and Bear: a Perfect Marriage," and "Basketball, Thoroughbreds, and FOOTBALL!" Good to have a beaming school president, Herman Donovan, standing next to him as he stood there addressing the raucous crowd.

Bear Bryant held his hands up to quiet them one more time.

"I know you've got great basketball – a tradition of winning you can be proud of. Well, now you're gonna be just as proud of your football team, too." The crowd erupted again and he waited patiently for them to simmer down enough so he could go on. "Kentucky is about to display a fire-and-brimstone style of play in another sport." More cheers. Even a few chants broke out toward the rear of the hall. "And we're gonna have championship trophies in that other sport, too. As of this day, there are now two championship sports on the University of Kentucky campus!"

It was clear from the reaction of the crowd that these words were exactly what they wanted to hear from their new coach. Still, their approval wasn't enough for him.

Bryant sought validation of his abrupt career move from someone he trusted – someone he knew would tell him exactly what he needed to hear. Not long after the introductory meeting with the students and boosters in Lexington, he headed back home to Tuscaloosa to visit with Coach Frank Thomas.

As he stepped into Thomas' office, Bear was surprised at how frail and tired the old coach appeared.

"Coach Tommy, I came down here for two reasons…to see how you're feeling and to see what you thought about my move."

The old coach smiled and studied the pictures on the wall of his office for a bit before he answered.

"Well, as for me, I'm pooped, Bear. But I think I've got a squad coming on that'll make me feel young again."

"That's some of that Fightin' Irish spirit I've always admired in you, Coach Tommy."

Thomas shook his head and laughed softly.

"I suppose. But if I didn't think this was another Rose Bowl-caliber outfit…well…I'd hang it up and let somebody younger take it over."

"You'll make it, Coach," Bear said, taking a long draw on his cigarette. He blew a cloud of smoke toward the ceiling. "The truth is, it's me I'm worried about."

Thomas looked him in the eye.

"That's the way it is with this profession, Bear. The thorn in the rose."

"Sir?"

Thomas smiled again.

"You did the right thing, Bear, leaving Maryland. You can't be a real leader anywhere that they won't let you be the boss."

"Well, what about Kentucky?"

"It's a perfect match…a program that's down and a confident coach who has players who'll work for him. That's what you're going to have to sell up there."

Bryant blew out another long breath and watched the smoke until it dissipated.

"They'll buy it, and we will win."

Thomas smiled again. There was a twinkle in his eye now.

"Yeah, but even as confident as you are, you have to know that you're going to get your fanny tanned at least one time this season."

Bryant returned the smile and waved his hand in the air.

"Aw, Coach Tommy, I couldn't beat you if we played every year for the next thousand years."

"Bear, you are correct when you say that Kentucky isn't Alabama when it comes to the game of football. But I'd be stupid to stay around after this year and run the risk of you and that bunch up there beating us next season and all the seasons to follow."

Bear didn't reply. He studied the front of the old coach's desk. But inside he felt his heart leap. Frank Thomas wouldn't say it if he didn't think it could happen.

And he had just sung Bear Bryant's favorite song.

Now all he had to do was convince his team that better times lay ahead of them. In the first meeting with his new flock of players, with the new staff sitting on the front row, Bear simply stood there for a moment, looking out at them as they all settled into their seats, ready to hear their new coach's first speech.

But instead of talking, Bryant first walked to the back of the platform, took a piece of chalk and deliberately scratched out some figures on a blackboard. The players craned their necks to see what he was doing and mumbled to each other.

"2-8," he wrote, then studied the numbers for a bit. Then he scrawled out "28-2." Only then did he put down the chalk and walk back to the front of the little stage.

"I assume you gentlemen know what that '2-8' means." The room was quiet. Several of the players squirmed uncomfortably in their seats. "But just in case, that's your won-loss record last season. And this other number…'28-2?'…That's what the Kentucky basketball team did this season. For now, it's the only record that matters to most of the folks in Lexington and Louisville. Am I right?"

Some of the players nodded weakly. No one spoke.

"Well, what about it? Am I right?"

"Yes, sir!" they loudly replied in unison.

"That's a hell of a lot better. Well, let me tell you all something. You will do better this year if you want it badly enough. And then they'll start to take notice that they have another program on this campus that deserves some attention, too. Hell, I know you feel like second-class citizens on campus. I'm not about to accept that! And neither should you. Because gentlemen, I've got the answer…simple but demanding. One that has been tested by time. We're all…you, me, the assistant coaches…gonna work our asses off to change the way people think about University of Kentucky football. And it isn't going to be long before you can hold your heads up, poke out your chests and be proud of who you are."

The room erupted in cheers. Bryant smiled and winked at his assistants. He…and they…knew the redirection of Kentucky football had just begun. And that making this bunch into winners would be no easy task.

Bear would soon find out just how difficult it would actually be.

It was late. Very late.

Bear eased down carefully onto the side of his bed and began unlacing his shoes. Mary Harmon abruptly sat up, yawned and looked sleepily at the clock on the nightstand.

3:20 AM.

"I'm sorry I woke you up," he apologized.

"Where in the world have you been?" she asked with another powerful yawn.

"At the office."

"Alone?"

"No. The staff was there with me."

Mary Harmon slipped from beneath the covers and eased across the bed to sit beside him.

"Paul, you might be asking too much too soon."

He dropped a shoe and looked at her sideways.

"Obviously, you think so."

"Well, Paul, some of the other coaches' wives are complaining already."

He was quiet as he turned off the lamp and slipped out of his clothes. She lay back down. He slid in beside her.

"I pay their husbands to work."

"But you're just starting here. You'll fizzle out if you don't slow down."

He suddenly sat up straight in the bed.

"Listen, Mary Harmon, every coach they've run off from Kentucky got fired for something other than his won-loss record. If they get rid of me, it's going to have to be because of losing. And I don't intend for that to happen. I've got a bunch of football players who need good guidance. I've got fans that are hungry for a team that's a winner. And I'm determined to provide for both of them."

She was quiet for a moment before she spoke again.

"No, Paul, you listen. It's early in the season, and you're tired already. Your staff is tired. Your players…"

"You're damn right I'm tired. But I'm not gonna feel tired in November when those basketball-crazy editors are finally trying to find space for football on the front of their sports sections."

With that, he fell back onto the pillow and was snoring quietly in less than a minute.

"Good night, Paul," Mary Harmon said, but she was now wide-awake.

It seemed as if everyone in the tiny little Kentucky town was packed into the cramped school cafeteria. The mayor – a squat, fat, bald man – had just waddled to the podium. He blew into the microphone and tapped it a couple of times, making sure it was on as he surveyed the crowd of players seated out front, their dates and parents and supporters, and the others who sat at the head table behind him. The room finally settled down. The mayor ignored the hint of feedback in the PA system as he spoke.

"Ladies and gentlemen, faithful citizens, welcome to our high school football banquet. It is my great pleasure to introduce our guest speaker for tonight, the University of Kentucky head football coach, Mr. Paul "Bear" Bryant. His first Kentucky team now has a 6-2 record with West Virginia and Tennessee still left to play. Folks, let's give a big welcome to Coach Bryant."

Bryant stood, walked to the podium, and then towered over the short little mayor as he acknowledged the cheers of the crowd. The mayor stretched to reach up to pat him on the back.

"Ordinarily, I'd give Coach Bryant a key to our city. But the truth is I gave the only one we had to Coach Adolph Rupp, our beloved basketball coach at UK, so I'm afraid I don't have one to offer." The crowd laughed politely, and the mayor smiled up at Bryant. He couldn't help noticing, though, the anger that flashed across his guest speaker's face. The mayor cleared his throat, took a step back, and said, "So…uh…I'll just present Coach Bryant."

Bear stood there, surveying the smiling, applauding throng, but his face was still rain cloud dark. When the clamor died away, he half turned to where the mayor was easing back into his chair at the head table behind him.

"Mr. Mayor, I appreciate your welcome, but I'm afraid I don't care much for your attempt at humor. You see, sir, by the time I'm finished at Kentucky, we'll have won enough in football for me to come back up here and buy you and your hick town." Bryant ignored the gasps and murmurs from the shocked crowd and the look of distress on the mayor's face. The coach finally smiled. "And if we win a Southeastern Conference championship, which I fully expect we will do… I might just retire here and take your job away from you."

The crowd went wild.

Many of the players on Bryant's first Kentucky team were former servicemen, only recently released by the Army or Navy. Their coach looked younger than most of them.

At the pre-game meal, Coach Bryant waved one of the waiters over to his table.

"I'd like a cup of coffee, please," the coach said.

"No. You'll have to have milk or tea, just like everyone else."

"Look, I want a cup of coffee," Bryant said, growing irritated.

"I'm sorry, the coach left word the players had to have milk or tea, and that's all I can let you have. I can check with him if you want me to."

Laughter erupted all around as the players and coaches realized the waiter's mistake. One of the war veterans stood and put his arm around the waiter's shoulder.

"It's all right. Let the boy have his coffee."

The place exploded again.

Out there on the practice field, storm clouds seemed to be flitting across the face of the Wildcats' coach as he impatiently watched his charges scrimmage. Finally, he was unable to take what he was seeing any longer. At the end of one play, he raced across the field and arrived at a pileup before the echo of the whistle had died out.

"No. No. No. Hell, no! That's not defense. I don't know what it is, but it's not defense. And it sure ain't football!"

He began yanking players from the pile and flinging them aside like cord wood until he finally got to a smallish defensive end who was lying on his back at the bottom of the stack. The coach grabbed his shoulder pads and pulled the player roughly to his feet, then seized fists full of the young player's bloody jersey and yanked him close, face to face. The youngster's cheeks and chin were smeared with blood. More of it dripped ominously from his nose.

"Damn, son," Bear yelled. "Look at you. You're all bloody because you're letting them beat you to death. You've got to learn to fight back, or you can just turn in your uniform."

But Bear saw something in the youngster's eye then. A flash of something. And the player's voice was determined when he said, "Yes, sir!"

"All right, then. Get your ass down in a stance and try to block me, and I'll show you how to play defense."

The end looked around, his eyes wide, searching for confirmation from someone that he had just heard right…that his head football coach had told him to try to knock him on his butt.

But Bear was already positioned in a three-point stance, nodding toward an assistant coach. The young player quickly dropped down and tried to square away against Bryant.

The assistant barked the count, "Down! Set! Hut!"

On "Hut!" the coach fired forward as if propelled by a rocket, struck the player a mighty blow across the face with a forearm, easily knocked him aside with the other and then trotted past where the young defender lay on his back, looking up at the Kentucky-blue sky.

Bear turned to watch the player struggle back to his feet, stagger a bit, then shake his head to clear the haze.

"That's great. Tennessee just sacked our quarterback again."

But the young player tried to pull himself up, to stand taller, as he wiped the blood from his nose with the tail of his jersey.

"But I'll get better, Coach," he said. "I will get better."

"You will?"

"Yes, sir. I'll keep working till I get it right."

The coach walked back and put his arm across the player's shoulder pads.

"You have to get better, son, or we'll be picking you up off the ground in Knoxville with a shovel," he said.

Then, the coach heard a chuckle from one of the other players watching the scene play out. Bryant turned, his eyes narrowed, and he stepped quickly to where the player stood. The young man wasn't laughing any longer. All the color had left the player's face.

Bear grabbed the player by the neck of his jersey and pulled him nose-to-nose. Still, close as they were, when the coach spoke it was loud enough that everyone on the field could hear him.

"Listen to me. Don't you ever laugh at a teammate. I've been watching you wallowing around out here. And that little son of a bitch you're laughing at could probably whip your butt right now if I turned him loose on you."

No one else was laughing. The players seemed awe-struck. They had never seen a head coach get down and head-butt with them –

especially without benefit of helmet and pads – the way this crazy man had just done. Bryant let the player go with a hard shove that almost sent him backward onto the ground.

"The rest of you better realize right here and now that we're all in this together. If we don't come together as a team and take shape, we'll get destroyed during the fall." He looked from one player to another, noting whose eyes met his and whose were averted. "Do you understand that we are a team here at Kentucky?"

"Yes, sir!" the players responded, immediately and loudly.

The look in the eyes of the other players left no doubt. The coach was making believers out of them.

It was a bitter cold day. November, 1950. Gritty hominy snow peppered down, tossed about by a biting wind blowing in sharply off the Tennessee River. Even so, the stadium was full as the Kentucky and Tennessee teams warmed up on opposite ends of the gridiron.

At the far end of the field, beneath the goal post, Paul Bryant talked quietly with one of his assistants as they watched their team shake out the kinks of the trip down from Lexington. Bear nodded toward the opposite end zone, squinting to see through the fog of peppering snow.

"Well, there's The General. As much as I despise him, I guess I oughta go shake his hand."

They could just make out the form of Coach Bob Neyland, watching his own team get ready for the big showdown.

"Bear, he's won four in a row over us, but we're better than them this year. I think it's time to shoot down the buzzard."

"Damn, Carney, don't forget the tie. I'm worried enough without you adding to the humiliation. Besides, all this snow and ice and wind are liable to disarm Parilli. And if we can't pass, we can't beat 'em."

"We'll out-will Tennessee this time, Bear. Nobody wants to beat anybody any worse than we want to whip their tails. When we're finished today, the Sugar Bowl and the Rose Bowl both are gonna want us."

Paul Bryant scowled at his assistant.

"You're forgetting something, Carney. We're third in the nation in the polls, but we still don't have a firm bowl invitation."

"We will when we beat this bunch!"

"Yeah, but we ain't beat 'em yet."

Three hours later, a dejected Bear Bryant walked to the middle of the field. Bob Neyland was coming his way, triumphantly borne on the shoulders of his players. Bryant's face remained somber as he completed the obligatory congratulatory handshake and turned to head back to the locker room and his defeated team. A wild-eyed Vol fan ran up, jumped in front of him and brazenly taunted him.

"You can't beat The General, Bear. You oughta know that by now! You can't even get one win against Tennessee!"

The fan pointed toward the scoreboard as the police escort shoved him out of Bear's way. Bryant paid no attention to him. Still, as he walked on, he considered the sad news displayed by the scoreboard for all to see.

"There'll come a time," he muttered under his breath. "Dammit, there'll come a time against this bunch."

Two hours later, at a nearby hotel restaurant, Bear sat across the table from Charlie Zatarain, who represented the Sugar Bowl selection committee. Despite the great meal before them, both men wore long faces, and the conversation between them had been sparse so far. Bryant finally slid back, lit a cigarette and asked the question he had been sitting on for the better part of an hour.

"Charlie, what's the selection committee thinking by now?"

He waited for Zatarain to take a sip of his wine before he answered.

"Well, Bear, I expect you know the answer. Your loss this afternoon threw a real wrench into the works, and everybody is upset. We wanted Kentucky and Oklahoma in a battle of unbeatens. We don't have that match up any more."

Bryant chewed on the cigarette then pulled it from his lips and pointed the fiery end in the general direction of Zatarain.

"Let me tell you about upset. I sent a damn good football team to the airport a little while ago, and every player on that bus was crying. And if the damn officials knew the rules of the game, we would still be unbeaten."

"I know, Bear, but Wyoming still is undefeated. And with Oklahoma on a 31-game winning streak, well…"

"That's enough, Charlie. Let's go get your bosses on the phone right now. And I don't give a damn if you have to call everybody in New Orleans."

Upstairs in Zatarain's hotel room, the Sugar Bowl rep was in the process of placing the call when there was a rap at the door. Bryant waved for him to keep working on getting someone on the line as he answered the knock. It was Bernie Moore, the commissioner of the Southeastern Conference.

"What's the deal?" he asked.

Bear gave him a weak grin.

"Come on in, Bernie. I'm about to make the sales pitch of a lifetime."

Zatarain waved at Moore, spoke into the phone mouthpiece, then motioned Bryant closer.

"OK, Coach, you wanted him. This is the chairman of the committee."

Bear took the phone, looked at it for a moment, took a deep breath, and then put the instrument to his ear.

"Before you say anything, let me tell you I'm a lynched coach if I don't land this Kentucky team in a bowl game." He paused, listening to the reaction of the man on the other end of the phone line. "I know that, and you know that. What you don't know...and apparently don't believe...is that we'll kick Oklahoma's ass if you'll just give us a chance to play them in the Sugar Bowl."

Zatarain and Moore looked at each other and tried to stifle their laughter. Bear ignored them and went on with his sales pitch.

"Damn right, I know what I said. And hell, I don't care if you tell every reporter in America that I guaranteed a victory over the Sooners." Bryant listened some more. Then his face cracked into a broad grin. "That's fine with me. And I promise you this. I'll build this game up so big nobody else will even care that the Rose Bowl is being played the same day."

He placed the phone back on its cradle, turned toward the other two men in the room, and, with a broad grin, told them, "Gentlemen, on New Year's Day, the Big Blue is going to be playing Oklahoma in the Sugar Bowl in New Orleans." He checked his wristwatch. "And I'm going to the train station."

Later, as the train raced across the dark, snowy countryside, Bear sat quietly, looking out the window, thinking about how far he had come since he helped his folks work that river bottom land back in Arkansas. He remembered a time when he was cutting up in church, only to have his mother get up in the middle of the sermon, grab him by the arm and pull him out of the sanctuary in front of everyone, taking him outside to give him a good switching. He never acted up in church after that.

Then, he recalled the time he drove a wagon filled with ten pigs away from the farm, bound for town. On the way, when he tried to cross a rain-swollen creek, it had been all he could do to save the wagon and its cargo, urging the mules to swim with all their might to get them out of the flooded stream and to dry ground on the other side.

As he watched the moon shining on the cloak of white snow outside the train window, he thought of happier times, too. Of him and Mary Harmon, walking hand-in-hand across the quad at the University of Alabama, listening to the peal of Denny Chimes, pretending it was a private serenade just for the two of them.

And he pictured himself, standing in the doorway of his children's bedroom in College Park, Maryland, watching Mae Martin and Paul Jr. as they peacefully slept, unaware of the turmoil that swirled all around them – the uproar that was part of a coach's life.

"Excuse me, Coach Bryant." The interruption startled him, but the man seemed friendly enough. It was a man and a woman, two Kentucky fans, still wearing their blue outfits. Their faces were still ruddy and pinched from the chapping, cold wind in Knoxville…or maybe from the tears of defeat. "We just wanted to tell you we are sorry about how the game turned out. We were robbed."

"But don't worry about that, Coach," the woman fan added. "You've restored something important to us. You've given us back our pride in football."

"Now, if we just had a bowl game to play in, this all might be a little bit easier to swallow," the male fan said sadly.

Bryant smiled up at them.

"I'll let you folks in on a little secret." He motioned them to lean closer. "You might just want to buy yourselves a couple of tickets to New Orleans before you leave the station tonight."

"Oklahoma?" the woman loudly asked, eyes wide in disbelief.

Bear motioned for her to be quiet, but a grin split his face when he told her, "Uh huh. And Sugar, we're gonna whip their tails."

The game was as hard fought as everyone predicted. With just over ten minutes left to go, Kentucky led Oklahoma 13 to 0.

Across the stadium, the Kentucky faithful pleadingly chanted, "Dee-fense! Dee-fense! Dee-fense!"

Down on the sidelines, Bear Bryant paced nervously, wishing he could light up a Chesterfield and go ahead and celebrate this victory. But it was much too early for that. He had tinkered with the defense, using a scheme different from anything the 'Cats had run that season. They had been running a nine-man line to halt Oklahoma's powerful wide option game. It had worked wonderfully, so far, but he knew his team was now playing mostly on heart and guts. He had no idea how much longer they could keep that up.

The officials waved their arms, indicating a Sooner timeout. Defensive end Charlie McClendon trotted off the field toward his coach. The smallish defender bled from a cut on his cheek, but he took no notice of such a minor thing. No more notice than he had taken of his bloody nose years before, on that day at practice when Bear Bryant had used him like a tackling dummy to show the kind of defense he wanted to play at Kentucky.

"Don't worry, Coach. They'll never score on us twice," McClendon said with strong assurance.

"Okay, Charlie Mac, if you say it's so, I believe you. But tell your teammates that this is the glory they were working for back in August."

"I sure will."

McClendon winked at his coach, turned, and ran back toward the defensive huddle.

The victory party had been going on for quite a while already. Bear had danced at least a dozen dances with his bride, but now it was time to refill his glass at the bar. One of the Kentucky boosters joined him, clapping him on the back one more time.

"Son of a bitch, Coach," he hooted. "Every paper in America will have stories in the morning editions about Kentucky football."

Bryant took a long, thirsty drink from his newly filled glass.

"That's right, Jake. And we might just knock Rupp and his basketball boys to an inside page in Lexington for a change."

"Hell, The Baron won't like that."

Bryant fished in his jacket pocket for his pack of cigarettes.

"Well, he has tasted the spoils of victory long enough. Now it's our time." Bear pulled a fancy lighter from his trouser pocket and started to light the cigarette in his mouth with it, but he stopped and studied the thing for a moment, as if he might have just seen it for the first time. The tone in his voice changed when he spoke again. "You're right, Jake. But this lighter is proof of something we all know. And something we all hate to admit."

"I don't know what you mean, Bear."

"This is what I got after we won the SEC championship. They gave Coach Rupp a damn new Cadillac the last time he won it."

"Well, that's about to come to an end. He's gonna retire."

"Maybe so, maybe not," Bryant said as he continued to study the lighter, the cigarette in his lips so far unlit. "But I'm sure of one thing. I'm ready to retire…to some back room and shoot some craps."

Bear Bryant was lost in his work, sitting at his desk, drawing football plays on blank sheets of paper. He heard the two newspaper reporters as they passed his doorway. He looked up, but they were gone, apparently headed for someplace other than the head football coach's office. He shrugged his shoulders and went back to work.

But he couldn't ignore the conversation that started up in the hallway outside his door a moment later. They were all talking plenty loud enough for him to hear every word they said.

"OK, if you snoops want a good interview, let's get started."

It was the unmistakable voice of Adolph Rupp, the legendary head basketball coach at the University of Kentucky. And it sounded as if he was intent on holding a press conference right outside Bryant's door.

"Coach Rupp, we were wondering if…well…the rumors are that…"

"You snoops want to know if I'm quitting because of that points-shaving deal. Well, the answer is 'Hell, no!' I'm not leaving now and let that damn Bear Bryant turn Kentucky into a football factory."

The reporters laughed.

Bear Bryant lifted the fancy cigarette lighter from where the damnable thing was resting on his desk. He hurled it across the room toward the far wall.

It shattered into a dozen pieces upon impact.

The mint julep was cold and flavorful and refreshing all the way down. He ordered another one before the first one was half gone.

Mary Harmon Bryant, seated next to her husband, was absolutely radiant as she sipped her orange juice – far more beautiful than all the other VIPs in the Churchill Downs boxes.

The thoroughbreds were just making their way past them, headed for the starting gate and the running of the 1953 Kentucky Derby.

Bryant leaned closer to his bride.

"You better enjoy this one, Baby. It'll be our last one."

She gave him the look she reserved for those times when she was of the opinion that he was jumping the gun on something.

"Don't say that, Paul. This is the best place we've ever lived."

"You haven't heard those people behind us? They've been talking Kentucky basketball ever since we sat down here. And that's after we've had fifty-three wins in seven years."

"That's only natural. That points deal has everybody talking about basketball around here."

"That's exactly my point. Rupp's coming back next year, and they're going to be loaded." He took another sip of his mint julep. "I'm telling you, Mary Harmon, now's the time to make a move."

She pretended to be watching the prancing racehorses, straining to run free before they ever reached the orderly confinement of the starting gate. She seemed to be ignoring him.

But he knew she had heard him. And that she already knew for certain that it was time for them to pack up and move again.

Chapter Six:

To Hell and Back

Luring a coach of Paul Bryant's stature away from a good job at Kentucky to Texas A&M had been a priority of several members of the school's board of directors, especially its newest and youngest member, Jack Finney.

At the very first board meeting he attended, Finney told the chancellor, the president and the rest of the members exactly how he felt, mincing no words as he watched some of them squirm uncomfortably.

"We have the sorriest athletic program in the country, and I mean to do something about it."

It wasn't long before he and the board dispatched the A&M athletic director, Bones Irvin, to the national coaches convention on a mission to land Bear Bryant or someone like him to come to College Station.

"Bones, what did Coach Bryant say to our offer?" Finney asked the AD upon his return.

"Ain't interested."

"Not even when you explained to him that the job was both head coach and athletic director?"

Irvin shook his head. He was already athletic director. He had not known the position was going to be open.

Finney was on the telephone to Lexington, Kentucky, early the next morning, and he was in no mood to take "no" for an answer.

"Coach Bryant," he began. "We're thinking about contacting Johnny Vaught over there at Ole Miss about our coaching job, and I was wondering if you could tell us if he might be a good fit for our program."

"He's a pretty fair coach, all right," Bear answered, likely more than pleased with the prospect of getting Johnny Vaught whisked away from the conference.

"Well, I appreciate the information, Bear." Finney paused, prepared to set the hook. "I'm just sorry you didn't see fit to accept our offer to come on down here and be our coach and athletic director."

There was a moment's pause on the other end of the line. Bryant had taken the bait and was about to run with it.

"Nobody ever offered me the AD job," Bear finally said.

"Oh, yeah. That's the deal. Coach and AD. Now, about Coach Vaught…"

The fish was hooked.

"Whoa. That's a different deal."

"How much money would it take, Coach?"

"Whatever the school chancellor makes ought to be about right."

"We can do that. How many of the assistant coaches would you keep?"

Bryant didn't hesitate. "Not a one of 'em. I don't want anybody with me that's already gotten used to losing."

Finney leaned back in his chair and grinned.

He had reeled in the head football coach he had been angling for.

It was pure hot. The Texas sun beat down mightily, even though it was only June. W. T. Doherty, a member of the Texas A&M

University board of directors, steered the big car along the lone main street in College Station. Despite its size, the car seemed full of folks.

Bear Bryant rode in the front passenger seat. Mary Harmon shared the back seat with Mae Martin, now 17, and 9-year old Paul Jr.

"I don't think I've seen a place to shop yet," Mary Harmon whispered to her daughter.

"I haven't seen much of anything at all," Mae Martin whispered back.

"Bear, you can't get a better lunch in the world than you can get at that little bar over yonder," Doherty was saying. "Their cornbread makes the mouth water."

"I hope none of your football players hang out there."

Doherty chuckled.

"No way. I don't think we have any that are tough enough to drink more than two beers without passing out cold as a wedge."

Mary Harmon leaned forward and touched the school president on the shoulder.

"Excuse me, but where is the country club?"

"Well, we don't exactly have one like what you're probably accustomed to. But we do have some social events that you'll..."

"And you don't seem to have any places to shop either," Mary Harmon interrupted, then ignored her husband's sharp look from the front seat. Bryant had already noticed the wan complexion on his wife's face when she came down the stairs from the airplane, surveying their flat, hot new home.

"Mrs. Bryant, Houston is only a tad more than an hour away...maybe two in thick traffic."

Paul Jr. piped up with a question of his own: "Why do all those boys over there have on Army suits?"

Doherty chuckled.

"We're a military school, son, and you'll see a lot of marching because of it, like at noon tomorrow, when we introduce your daddy to the corps."

"Like playing war?" the youngster asked.

"Yep, or training for…"

"They are sort of cute," Mae Martin chimed in.

Doherty laughed again, as much at the expression on her daddy's face as at Mae Martin's observation.

"I'm glad at least two of you like what you see of A&M. And as for you others, believe me, Texas A&M will grow on you."

They rode on in silence for a few minutes, and then Bear asked, "Mr. Doherty, what exactly does your chancellor make?"

"I beg your pardon."

"I have to make about what the chancellor makes…and certainly more money than the head of your chemistry department."

Doherty scratched his head and steered the big car around a corner toward the athletic facilities.

"Well, Coach, that's a bit irregular."

"But I'm not a regular coach."

"With some corporate assistance, we'll arrange something for you. But what in the world made you think of such a thing?"

"Because, with all due respect, Mr. Doherty, your school appears to me to be in dire need of something it can rally around. And sir, it's impossible to rally around what's happening in some chemistry lab."

The next day just after noon, seated on a platform alongside the school president and with his family there behind him, Bryant watched the cadets march back and forth while the band played. He enjoyed the orderliness of it all, the discipline. But when the ranks finally formed up before the platform and the "At rest!" command was barked, one of the cadets screamed, "Beat the hell out of Texas!" Others joined in, and they all cheered wildly.

The president of the school, Dr. David Hitchens Morgan, approached the podium and waved his hands for order.

"Gentlemen, you know these people up here on the stage, so I won't bore you. I'll just present to you a great football coach, Paul 'Bear' Bryant."

The group of cadets erupted once more, whooping and cheering. Bryant stood there at the podium for a moment, watching the corps, listening to their acclaim, soaking it all in.

But suddenly, as if he had been seized by some force mightier than he, the coach sprinted to the front of the platform, ripped off his sport coat and flung it to the ground as if the coat had offended him mightily in some way. With a growl worthy of his name, he stomped on the garment and danced on it, all while the cadets urged him on.

Then he jerked the necktie from his throat, threw it on the floor as well, and danced on it just as vigorously. The crowd was beside itself by then. The president watched wide-eyed as his new football coach seemed to be having some kind of conniption fit.

But Bear wasn't finished. Next, the coach unbuttoned the sleeves of his dress shirt, frantically rolled them up to his elbows and shook his clenched fists in the general direction of Austin, the home of the University of Texas.

The crowd was in a frenzy by then.

Finally, he left the trampled coat and tie behind and stepped toward the microphone to speak.

"That's the message we're sending to those uppity so-and-sos from Texas…and to all the pompous so-and-sos at all the other places in this conference." He narrowed his eyes and looked into the faces of the gathered cadets. Even the school's president was smiling and clapping with them by now. "They've got to know that they won't have A&M to kick around any more. We're gonna get us some players and make sure that we are too damn tough for them to handle from now on." The coach dashed back to the front of the stage, stomped on the sport coat one more time and finally gave it a good kick before grabbing the microphone again. "And once we get 'em down, we're not gonna let 'em up. Not until A&M beats everybody in sight on the way to the Cotton Bowl!"

The sun wasn't even up good, but it was already stifling hot. Blazing hot. Better than a hundred young men had gathered in the rough mess hall for breakfast, and they were already sweating and grumbling. Several vowed to head back for the swimming hole once the morning practice was over.

Paul Bryant rose from the table where he and his staff were eating and walked deliberately to the middle of the room. The rattle of dishes and clanging of silverware died out as they all got ready to listen to what their coach was about to say.

"Boys, my advice to you would be to go light on that food. We're about to go to work out there." Several of the players chuckled. A couple ignored their coach's advice and shoveled more eggs and grits into their mouths. "In about an hour, you're gonna get a taste of football played the way it's meant to be played. You fellows who consider me to be a comedian might want to take a good look at your surroundings. There's not much to do out here except practice football, swim and eat. And I assure you we didn't bring you all the way out here so you could work on your suntans. So if I were you, I'd get ready to go to work. Go to work to get yourself ready to be a winner. If you last the next few days, if you show the kind of heart it's gonna take, then you will be a winner. And that's all I want around me, all I want on a team of mine…winners!"

The scene later that morning in the far corner of the rocky, nearly grassless practice field was typical. Three players were blocking a single defensive lineman in a drill. On the assistant coach's cry of "Hut!" they buried the defender, piling on top of him there amid the rock and gravel and sandspurs. After the whistle, they unpiled, and the defensive lineman stayed down, writhing in the dust, groaning in agony. The assistant coach stood over him, screaming.

"Get your fat ass up! Get up and fight back, you lazy slob!" The three blockers watched, a pained expression on their faces, as the assistant bent over the fallen player. "You gonna get up, or are you gonna quit?"

"Quitting," came the muffled reply.

"What?"

"I'm quitting."

"Then get that uniform off, get your stuff packed and get out of here!"

A few days later, another player limped away from another similar scene. His knees seemed wobbly, and he held his stomach with both hands. Suddenly, he dropped to his knees and retched.

Nothing came up. Nothing was left.

A young newspaper reporter named Mickey Herskowitz stood nearby, watching as the player finally struggled back to his feet and plodded on toward the makeshift dressing room.

The reporter fell into step beside him.

"Tom, would you say things have changed with A&M football?"

"I'll say one thing. I hate that bastard. He's the meanest son of a bitch in history."

"Is The Bear that bad?"

"You count the members of the squad that's left. Somebody said nearly 40 have left already in just a couple of days. I'm about to make it 41."

Not far away, a smallish halfback was attempting to run the football through a gauntlet of tacklers. He was hammered to the ground. He remained there when the mob of tacklers climbed off the top of him. An assistant coach ambled over and looked down at him.

"Damn, Bud. I don't know if you're dead or alive." The halfback didn't move for a moment, but then finally nodded his head. "Then get up and run it again. Them Longhorns will tackle you a hell of a lot harder than these galoots just did." The halfback still could only lie there, barely moving as he sucked in hot, dusty air. "It's your last chance, Bud. Get up and run the ball, or you're gone."

The player rolled over onto his back.

"Then I guess I'm gone," he gasped. "Gone home. And I'm telling everything that's been going on out here."

The assistant coach pointed a finger at the player and grinned.

"Son, the only thing you'll be able to tell anybody is that Bear Bryant exposed your yellow streak."

When it was too dark one evening to practice any longer, Bryant herded what was left of his squad off the field, ordering them to run at a sprint all the way to the showers, assuring them that it would be tough to run hard in the fourth quarter against the Longhorns, too. Mickey Herskowitz fell in step beside the coach. He pointed back behind them, to where three or four players still lay on the rough, dusty practice field. None of them appeared to be moving.

"Reckon we ought to get the trainer to see about 'em?" he asked.

"Not unless he has some guts in his bag," Bear fired back at him without hesitation.

"You mind if I write that? It's a good angle for a story."

"Write anything you want to, Mick. But make sure you're honest and complete. Let your readers know that we're not being brutal like some of the papers are saying...that we're just teaching the Texas

A&M players to win. That's all we want. If they ain't winners, we don't need 'em."

Late that evening, three players crept through the rows of beds, making their way to the outside and back home, just as many of their teammates had done already.

"Damn, we're free at last," the lead player whispered as they stepped out into the still-sweltering night air.

"I know. But I ain't never quit a thing in my life," the one closest behind him said.

"Yeah, but nobody ought to have to put up with this hell."

They reached the end of the barrack and were about to scamper across the open ground to the road that led to the bus station. But one of them, the player who had never quit before, stopped and leaned back against the wall. The rough board siding felt cool through the sweat that soaked the back of his t-shirt.

"Hey, Powell, what are you doing?" the leader asked.

"Guys, I'm not a quitter. I'm going back and stick it out with the rest of 'em."

"You might not be a quitter, but you are one big fool."

"Maybe so. But it's for damn sure I'll be the best conditioned fool in the world once we leave Junction."

Not far away, Bear Bryant sat on the cot in his room, smoking, talking with his trainer, Smokey Harper, as he studied a list of players. He squinted through the smoke and sweat in his eyes as he considered the names that were crossed off the roster. He had already watched several more the shadowy figures make their escape this night.

"How many we got left by now?"

"Well, sir, let's see. You gonna take back that fat all-star center that up and quit?"

"What the hell do you think? Smokey, you're smart enough to know that a man who bails on me and the team now will quit in a snap against Texas."

"Then we've got about thirty of the damndest non-quitters known to mankind still with us when we open the season."

"And that's if nobody else walks off tonight," Bryant added. "Smokey, we didn't waltz into this thing, and we're not about to waltz out of it."

"But Bear, we open the season soon. Reckon you're gonna have enough left to field a team?"

Bryant considered some of the names left on the list. Jack Pardee. Dennis Goehring. Gene Stallings. Sometimes it was better to go to war with a hardened bunch than with a whole infantry of light-weights.

"We'll go with what we got. We're not building for this year. We're building the foundation for a championship down the line." He snuffed out the cigarette butt and rolled over onto the cot. He studied the ceiling for a bit then said, "They may not realize it yet...not the players or the administration or the boosters...but they will see what we are doing someday. They'll know then what we built out here."

Chapter Seven:

Bending the Rules

The scoreboard screamed the story: "Texas 22, Texas A&M 13" with just over a minute left to play. On the sidelines, Paul Bryant stood in the midst of his meager squad, watching the time click off far too slowly to suit him.

A disgusted player just off the field slammed his helmet down, almost at his coach's feet.

"Damn those bastards!" he screamed, but then realized his coach was watching him throw his fit. He picked up the headgear. "Sorry, Coach."

"That's all right, son. It's supposed to make you mad as hell when you lose."

"But we only won one game all year."

"Then we'll take what we learned from this season, and we'll build on that one win."

The player kicked the ground again and said, "I've learned one thing. We need more players if we mean to kick some tails."

Bryant pursed his lips and nodded agreement as he watched the last seconds melt away off the clock. He couldn't argue. The player was absolutely right. It was

hard to compete against the best in college football with such a small squad, no matter how devoted and hard-nosed they might be.

Weeks later, Bryant sat in a meeting room, surrounded by eight assistant coaches gathered around a large conference table. On the chalkboard at the far side of the room was a long list of names, headed by the word "Prospects." There were only a few check marks next to any of the names.

Bryant pointedly dropped a newspaper he had been reading on the table and slammed his fist down hard on top of it.

"The funny boys at the typewriters are trying to kill us. They're printing Aggie jokes every day, rehashing each of the losses like it's the funniest thing they ever saw." Bear leaned back in his chair and surveyed the other men around the table. "Boys, they're kicking us while we're down."

"It ain't any better out there on the recruiting trail," one of the assistants offered mournfully.

"That's for sure," added another. "The other recruiters are even making fun of us for taking that one-armed kid from Alabama."

"That young man's gonna be a helluva player," Bear grumbled. The one-armed player was Murray Trimble. He would later make all-conference as a guard, in his sophomore year at A&M. His younger brother, Wayne, would one day play for Bryant at Alabama.

"I'll tell you something else," the first coach said. "Every one of 'em that's giving us hell is paying players left and right. And especially them Baptists from Baylor and the Methodists from SMU."

"You sound sure about that," Bear said.

"You better believe it," another coach chimed in. "This ain't the SEC, Coach. Money rules in the Southwest. Oil and cattle money."

"Don't kid yourself," Bear said with a smile. "It happens in the SEC, too."

"But not like it does out here."

"Amen," several of the coaches agreed.

Bear Bryant leaned forward in the chair and slapped the table again.

"Then I tell you what we're gonna do. We're gonna match Baylor and SMU dollar for dollar…do what it takes to give A&M a fair chance."

"I don't know about that, Coach. Them other schools already have the NCAA watching us like hawks."

"That's the truth," another coach added. "They act like the good guys, and they've got the NCAA thinking we're the crooks."

Bear's eyes had gone steely, and his jaw was set firmly.

"Okay then, let's act the part and see if we can get some of those A&M oil barons to let loose some of that money."

"Bear, I'm afraid a lot of that oil money dried up after we went 1 and 9."

"I'll handle the fat cats. You boys just find me some players," Bear said through clenched teeth. "We're good enough to win with what we've got, but I don't want to take any chances. We'll outbid the rest of the bastards now, and then we'll out hit 'em come the fall."

The meeting was over.

Later that day, Jones Ramsey, the A&M sports information director, knocked on the coach's door. He was a big man, six-four and near 280 pounds.

"Come on in, it's open," the coach called. Ramsey walked in and sat down, waiting for Bryant to finish up the paperwork he was poring over. Without even glancing up, Bear said, "I swear, Jones, you look like you've been hitting that Mexican food harder than usual."

"Yep, it's full of calories, as well as being extra tasty."

"Same as whiskey."

"Well, Coach, you sort of wiped out my supply of that, so I wouldn't know."

"As I recall, I had some help on that."

"Well…but Coach, something tells me you didn't call me up here to talk about my weight problem and dietary habits."

Bryant finally looked up at the SID. He slid back in his chair, so he could put his feet up on the desk.

"I reckon you've heard what the Southwest Conference has gone and done. Put in a rule that outlaws off-site training camps like our deal out in Junction."

"Yes, sir. Seems like they're picking on us more than somewhat."

Bear snorted and studied the end of his cigarette for a moment.

"Jones, what's the alumni thinking?"

Ramsey considered the question for a moment then said, "The loyal ones are up, but the deadbeats are down. And there's considerably more of the latter."

"What about the rich ones?"

"Most are running the other way after this season."

"Then here's what we will have to do. We're going to embarrass them back into the fold with one of the all-time great press releases." Bryant flipped the page and handed Ramsey the legal pad he had been scribbling on. "You word it anyway you want to, Jones, but this is what it has to say. And present it as my quote."

"Fire away."

"Last year, I had a lot of people coming around saying, 'Hey, Bear, how's our team coming along?' Now, when they come around…if they do…they say, 'Coach, how's your team doing?' I'm shocked. That's not the Aggie spirit I've always heard about."

Ramsey pondered the notes he had scratched out on the legal pad.

"And?"

"That's it. You're a good enough publicity man to pad it."

Ramsey broke into a big grin.

"Coach, I know those folks. This'll work like a charm because it'll make 'em feel guilty."

"It better, Jones, because if it doesn't, I'll be plowing behind a mule again in no time."

Ramsey stood and headed for the door but stopped and turned around before he left the room.

"Where did you come up with this?"

Bryant smiled.

"I stole it from Frank Howard. He dusts it off and uses it every time the alumni at Clemson get too restless."

Jones laughed and went off to write his press release.

The expression on Dr. Morgan's face was grim as he sipped his coffee and appeared to be searching for the right words to begin the conversation. Paul and Mary Harmon Bryant were quiet as they drank from their cups of coffee. They were seated on the couch in their living room, but it was clear the visit to their home by the school president wasn't a social one. The small talk was over, and all three knew it was time to get to the crux of the meeting.

Morgan pointedly set his cup down and cleared his throat.

"Paul, this isn't the type conference meeting Texas A&M is supposed to be having. We've got the wolves after us."

"I'm sorry, Mr. President."

"Well, tell me what you know about all this."

"It's the truth. Some of our oil men gave a few prospects some money." Bryant set his cup on the coffee table in front of him. There was a pained look on his craggy face. He looked the president in the eye. "They've got us locked up if they want us."

"So you did know about it."

"Sort of, yes. But not all the details."

Mary Harmon couldn't stay quiet any longer.

"The other schools are as guilty as we are," she said. "Baylor and Texas, the whole lot of them for that matter."

"But they're not on probation," Morgan told her. "We are. As of today. And I'm embarrassed about the whole thing."

"So what do we do?" Bear asked, the anguish still obvious on his face.

"We'll have a press conference, and we'll accept the blame. Me and you. And we'll point some fingers while we're at it."

"Now you're talking," Mary Harmon said. "Name all of them. Let people know what's been going on."

Bear Bryant slid forward on the couch and pointed at his president.

"And we'll also tell them that they better watch out. That A&M can win without having to cheat. There might've been a time when we had to, just to get in step with everybody else. But Mr. President, A&M doesn't have to do that anymore. I've already told my coaches and players and even some of the alumni. Anybody who wants to take money to play ain't worth a damn anyhow. Mr. President, it won't ever happen again, and you can write that down."

The tall, lanky high school quarterback was helping Mary Harmon Bryant finish up the dinner dishes. Since it was her kitchen, she washed and he dried. As they worked, they chatted comfortably. But then Don Meredith was quiet for a few minutes. Mary Harmon knew precisely what was on his mind, but she waited and allowed him to say it out loud.

"Mrs. Bryant, I want you to know how thrilled I am being here," he finally said. "And that meal...well, I'm not sure my mama could match it."

"Then maybe we have what it takes to make sure you don't get

Sportswriter Al Browning with Alabama football coach Paul "Bear" Bryant. Browning helped plan the coach's funeral.

Sportswriter Al Browning greeting legendary former Alabama coach Wallace Wade.

Coach Bryant on the University of Alabama campus in the early 1960s, not long after "mama called him home."

Even though it was late in his career, Coach Bryant still did not hesitate to come down from his tower and show players how it should be done.

Bear Bryant takes a moment to give a fan an autograph.

Coach Bryant visits with John David Crow, who won the Heisman Trophy while playing for Bear at Texas A&M and was one of the coach's favorite players.

Golf was one of the coach's favorite pastimes, and he played with many of the game's best, as well as in numerous celebrity tournaments.

Coach Bryant at his favorite spot before a game...
leaning against the goal post.

Coach Bryant and the love of his life, Mary Harmon.

Georgia head coach Vince Dooley, former Bama star Joe Namath, and Coach Bryant.

Coach Bryant making a presentation to the widow of Dr. Pat Trammell. Pat was another of the coach's favorite players.

A familiar publicity photo of Coach Bryant in the 1970s, a time when his Crimson Tide was regularly winning national college football championships.

Paul Bryant as a player at the University of Alabama.

Ralph "Shug" Jordan, head football coach at Auburn, chats with Coach Bryant prior to another "Iron Bowl" in Birmingham.

Coach Bryant in a candid moment.

The coach in his familiar coaching tower on Thomas Field in Tuscaloosa. Players dreaded when Bryant came down to the field to straighten out someone he thought was not practicing hard enough or was running a play wrong.

Coach Bryant chats with former Alabama coach Wallace Wade, who took three different Crimson Tide teams to the Rose Bowl from 1923 to 1930. Bear greatly admired Coach Wade's work ethic and, obviously, his success at Alabama.

The Bear watches his team warm up prior to a night game.

President John F. Kennedy watches the 1963 Orange Bowl, won by Alabama 17-0 over the Oklahoma Sooners. The president watched one half from the Alabama side of the stadium and the other from the Oklahoma side.

President John F. Kennedy flips the coin before the start of the 1963 Orange Bowl game, in which Alabama defeated Oklahoma 17-0. Only a one-point loss early in the year to Georgia Tech kept Alabama from its second straight national championship. (Number 54 is team captain and All-American Leroy Jordan, playing in his final game at Alabama.)

A commemorative tray saluting the 1975 Auburn-Alabama game. Paul Bryant was a longtime spokesperson for Coca Cola, which sponsored his weekly statewide television show.

homesick when you come to play for Texas A&M," she said with a wink and a smile.

"Ma'am, I'll be honest with you. I've never seen a place like this. I'm just a country boy from Mount Vernon, out in the sticks."

She handed him the last dinner plate.

"Then you're a natural to play for Paul. His background is about as country as they come."

"I know that, but there doesn't seem to be much for a young man to do around here." He placed the plate in the cabinet and looped the dishtowel over its hanger. "Other than Mae Martin, I haven't seen a girl in two days."

She laughed.

"I know, Don. I cried for three days after we moved here. But believe me, this place will grow on you."

She tried to look into the young man's eyes then, but he had turned to head into the living room where a baseball game was on the television set, and Coach Bryant waited.

A month later, it was Coach Bryant doing the visiting, sitting in the big easy chair in the living room of the home of Don Meredith in Mount Vernon, Texas, two hours east of Dallas. The quarterback and his girlfriend sat together across from him on the couch.

The young prospect held a worn, old football in his lap. He fiddled with the frayed laces until he knew it was time for them to talk about something besides the crops and weather.

"Coach Bryant, this is the first football my dad bought me," he said.

"What were you? About eight years old?"

It was the girlfriend that answered, "No, sir. Don was only seven."

"Goodness gracious! I didn't even know what a football was until I was twice that old. But I'm sure glad Don knew."

Meredith dropped his head and intently studied the dangling seams on the well-used football, suddenly quiet again. Bryant noticed the change in his mood, but the girlfriend quickly picked up the slack in the conversation.

"What position did you play in college, Coach?"

"I was an end, but not a very good one. But I didn't come all the way up here to talk about my playing days. I came to get the best quarterback in Texas." He looked hard at Meredith. "But son, I got a feeling I made a trip for nothing."

Meredith set the ball aside, and his girlfriend stood and left the room. Bryant could see the tears forming in the youngster's eyes, then rolling down his cheeks.

"Coach, I'm sorry. I'm going to sign with SMU. But I would rather play for you."

Bryant didn't hesitate.

"Then you'd better get on down to College Station."

"Coach, if you were anywhere else but A&M..."

Bryant leaned back in his chair and crossed his legs.

"Son, I'll accept your decision. And I don't doubt you'll be a star at SMU."

"Thank you, sir. That's a high..."

"But son, you're gonna get your ass whooped when you tangle with Texas A&M."

"I'm sorry, Coach. If you were only at Arkansas. Or Kentucky. Or Alabama."

But Bryant didn't seem to hear him.

"Naw, it might not happen this season. But we're gonna whip SMU and everybody else we play. And I'm here to tell you that those down-and-out Aggies are about to play football the old-fashioned way."

Then the coach stood, shook the young man's hand and went off to tell the quarterback's mama how much he had enjoyed the fine meal she had prepared for him that evening…and that he would be getting on back down to College Station.

He had lots of work to do.

It was a beautiful scene. The A&M cadets seated behind the bench were counting down the last few seconds of the game: "Five…four…three…two…one." Then they happily stormed the field when the ending gun was fired.

The public address announced the story, and it echoed around the packed stadium for all to hear.

"We hope you enjoyed the game and will drive safely home. Final score, Texas A&M 21, Rice 7."

Paul Bryant couldn't keep the broad grin off his face as he made his way through the bedlam toward the middle of the field. His players whooped and hollered all around him, enjoying to the utmost this latest win in a glorious season.

He met the Rice coach, Jess Neely, at midfield and exchanged handshakes.

"Nice job, Jess. Your boys played hard today," he yelled to be heard over the boisterous celebration around them.

"Just not hard enough," Neely replied. "You've got a good team."

"Thanks, partner."

But Neely wasn't finished. He held onto Bryant's hand as he went on.

"Too bad the NCAA won't let you take them to a bowl game. I guess those are the wages of sin."

Bryant dropped the other coach's hand and glared at him.

"Yeah, I guess so. But I'd think you'd worry more about your own damn business and less about mine."

Then he turned and hurried off to celebrate with his team.

It was later that night before Paul Bryant could finally unwind enough to enjoy the victory. He was in their living room with Mary Harmon, Mae Martin and Paul Jr., finishing up the last of a bowl of ice cream and cake.

Mary Harmon could sense that something still bothered her husband.

"This one meant a lot, didn't it?" she asked.

"Uh huh," was his answer.

"And even more because Rice has that 'holier than thou' attitude."

Paul looked up at her then, the fire still flickering in his eyes.

"Yep, and that damn Neely had the gall to say what he did at the end."

"What'd he say, Papa?" Paul Jr. asked from where he lay in the floor, finishing up his own dessert.

"Nothing worth repeating."

Mae Martin jumped in.

"Well, I'm just glad I got home in time to see the game. And it's really something how the students are talking about a championship."

"But Houston tied us," her brother pointed out.

"That's just one blemish, Paul," his dad said. "If we can get Texas, that'll wrap up something the Aggies have wanted for what seems like a lifetime."

"And that'll be our bowl game," Mary Harmon said with a smile.

"Maybe so, Baby. Maybe not."

"The NCAA said we couldn't go. Seems like they'd have the last word."

Bryant grinned.

"Yeah, and I said maybe so, but maybe not."

The mood was electric at the pep rally the night before the Texas game. The traditional gigantic bonfire seemed to light up most of southeast Texas. The band played and the crowd, cognizant of the fact that their team actually had a chance to clinch the conference championship the next day, were ready to celebrate right through the game and beyond.

Still, their football coach had little trouble getting them to quiet down enough for him to say a few words. But what he said did nothing but set them off again.

"We've heard the jokes long enough. Now it's time for the jokes to be on Texas, not A&M!"

He finally had to wave his arms to get them to simmer down again.

"Hey, there's something else I'd like to say. As you know, the NCAA has banned us from a bowl game." A chorus of boos filled the chill night air. Bryant motioned for them to listen. "Well, I've got news for them and all those other schools that think Texas A&M is going to take this sitting down. When we beat Texas tomorrow…when we win the conference championship…we're going to a bowl game of our own." The crowd murmured curiously. What had Bear just said? How was such a thing possible? "I've arranged for our team to play Hawaii in Honolulu on January 1."

The crowd exploded as the band kicked off the school fight song.

But things didn't look quite so bright the next morning before the game, as Bryant visited in the team hotel with Dr. Morgan. Morgan had the morning paper folded on his lap, and his expression was grim.

"Bear, listen to me. The NCAA has rules for members, and dammit, we're still a member."

"Well, Dr. Morgan, you've got to admit it was a good try. It's obvious to me Honolulu is a much nicer place to be on January first than Dallas."

"Maybe so, but now you've got to tell the players the deal is off…that there won't be another game after today."

Bryant studied the seam of his trousers for a long time before he replied.

"I don't agree with your decision, Dr. Morgan, but you are the boss, and I have to honor your request. And don't worry about the players. Let's just keep this conversation between us for right now, and I'll have them ready to get after the Longhorns."

It had become a familiar scene, but this one was especially glorious. The cadets and fans cheering. The team slapping each other on the back as the clock wound down. A&M on top at the end of a big game. The scoreboard blinking the beautiful story: "Aggies 34, Longhorns 21."

Coach Paul Bryant greeted each member of his kicking team as they trotted off the field and then turned to a group of team members standing behind him.

"Now we're kicking ass! Now we've got 'em licked! Now the jokes will be about Texas!"

The players yelled and whooped their agreement.

Then Bryant noticed one player, number 44, John David Crow, sitting on the bench by himself. He walked over to his star halfback, leaned forward and put his hands on his knees. He smiled and talked loudly to be heard over the throng already counting down the last few seconds of this latest triumph for the Aggies.

"Son, I don't know what those Heisman Trophy voters will say…they don't seem to favor juniors. But in my book, you are the best college football player in America."

Crow looked up, a broad grin on his face.

"Thanks, Coach. And looks like you're fast becoming the best coach." Bryant waved off the compliment and headed back to the sideline. "Hey, Coach!" Crow shouted. Bryant turned back. "And we might have the best team in America, too."

Bryant grinned, winked and headed back to his spot in front of the winning team bench.

He wanted nothing more than to savor the final sweet minutes of victory.

Chapter Eight:

Mama Calls

The cocktail party was in full swing, but the two men wandering through the crowd didn't seem interested in pressing the flesh with the others who were gathered there. Instead, they were obviously looking for someone else among the tuxedo-clad group.

One of the men suddenly pulled up short and tapped his friend on the shoulder. Young Boozer was a former teammate of Bryant's. He pointed toward the opposite end of the room.

"There's our buddy over there, Red. Right where I figured he'd be."

Red Blount was a businessman and a prominent supporter of the Alabama Crimson Tide. He looked in the direction Boozer was indicating. Sure enough, there was Paul Bryant, drink in hand, standing right next to a portable bar.

"Once a hell-raiser, always a hell-raiser," Blount said with a laugh.

They waved to the coach and made their way through the throng. Before he even said hello, Bryant turned to the bartender and told him, "Partner, fix up a couple of Black Jacks on the rocks." He extended his hand to each man in turn. "Boys, ya'll are looking good."

"And you do, too, Paul," Blount responded. "At least for an old football coach at war with the NCAA."

Bryant set his empty glass down and picked up a fresh one from the bar.

"Don't get me started on the NCAA. That bunch tries to use the same rules for a little bitty school that's lucky to get 5,000 people to come out for a game as it does for places like Texas A&M or Alabama that fill up those big stadiums. You know, I can't even buy a high school coach a sandwich or give him a ticket to one of our ball games, and Lord knows, A&M can afford that." He stirred the drink with his finger and took a big swig. "Okay, that's enough of that. We're here for a party, not to talk about the NCAA."

Boozer tipped his glass in the coach's direction. "I'm for that, Paul. But let's find a quiet place to talk about something else."

"Talk about what?"

Blount said, "A business proposition we have for you."

"Not tonight, Red. This is a football gathering, not a Wall Street meeting."

"It's football we want to talk to you about," Boozer said.

"Football in Tuscaloosa," Blount added.

The two Alabamians steered Coach Bryant through the crowd, out a doorway, and to a couch in the elevator lobby.

"So tell me, Paul, are you ready to come on down to Tuscaloosa and straighten things out?" Blount asked, point blank.

"They still want me after I turned them down the last time?"

Boozer didn't hesitate with his answer. "Damn right! And it has to get done quickly. We got fans threatening to go on strike."

"It's that bad?"

"You may not have noticed, being so busy coaching and fighting the NCAA, but Alabama didn't win a game last year, and we squeaked out just a couple of wins and a tie this year," Blount told him.

Boozer added, "And dammit, we've scored seven points on Auburn in three games. That won't do!"

"I'm aware of the record, men. It's my alma mater." Bryant studied his glass for a moment. "Tell me about the talent."

Young Boozer looked up from his almost-empty drink as he said, "Our 1934 team would beat them by a hundred points."

"But they've got pride," Blount was quick to add.

"How much longer has your coach got?"

"Next season, unless he pulls a miracle."

"But boys, I'd have to be the athletic director, too. And Coach Hank has that job. There's nobody on earth that I love more."

"We've got good plans for Coach Hank," Blount said.

"Then start getting some money together. And keep in mind that I've got a pretty sweet deal over there in Aggie land."

"That's understood," both men said.

"I'm telling you, Texas oil is a helluva lot more powerful than Alabama timber."

"You'll make more than any dean on campus," Boozer told him. "Plus a house and plenty more."

"Okay, I'll consider an offer. But I'm not just negotiating when I tell you A&M isn't bad. Those folks have been mighty good to me."

Boozer grinned.

"That's fine, Paul. But Red and I know one thing for certain. We know where your heart is."

The two businessmen told him goodbye and walked away to rejoin the party.

Paul Bryant sat there for a moment, swirling the ice around in the bottom of his glass, watching the dignitaries entering and leaving the lobby.

Tuscaloosa. The University of Alabama.

He remembered tossing the football back and forth to the other end on the team, All-American Don Hutson. Then briefly going into the laundry business with him, cleaning and pressing uniforms for the ROTC cadets on campus. Remembered sitting in meetings with his teammates, watching Coach Frank Thomas drawing plays on the chalkboard for them. Remembered working beside Coach Thomas as an assistant, drawing his own play on that chalkboard and then beaming when Coach smiled and told him it would work. Remembered walking across the quad with Mary Harmon, listening to the crickets until the chimes interrupted their song with its own serenade. The place was more home to him now than Fordyce or Moro Bottom. It was the place where he had come of age. Where he had made the sacrifices and commitment that put him on the path to where he was today.

Was it possible he would get the call? That he would be able to go back there to complete his career where he had started?

The dejected looks on the Aggie team's faces told all any observer needed to know about the outcome of the Gator Bowl game. Coach Bryant walked to a chalkboard at the far end of the locker room and everyone grew even quieter. They watched through teary eyes as he wrote: "24-5-2" on the board.

"Gentlemen, this is why you should be holding your heads up today. That's what you've done in three seasons. And given the circumstances, it's a damn good job." He surveyed the roomful of hurting players, most with their heads still bowed. "Let's get those heads up. Let's square those shoulders. Let's show some of that pride that you've brought back to A&M."

Several of the players yelled, "Yeah!" Some pounded others on their backs and shook hands. It was true. Every man knew that there was a new feeling now in the Aggie locker room. They had turned the program around. They had restored pride to Aggie land.

The coach moved back to the center of the room.

"Now, it's time for me to level with you. I know you've heard the rumors that I'm leaving A&M to go to Alabama. Well, gentlemen, it's true."

"You can't leave, Coach," one burly player yelled. "We're just getting a good start."

"That's true. And I wouldn't dream of going except for one important thing. You see, I sweated and bled for that program on the field of battle. It's where I got my start coaching. And there'll come a time when you will feel the same for A&M. It's..."

"But Coach, you gotta stay," the big player shouted. "You've got to help us bury Texas!"

"I can't do that, son," the coach said. "Alabama needs me. Mama has called me home."

The entire family gazed out the windshield as Paul Bryant steered the car down the last mile into Tuscaloosa. Even Doc, the family dachshund, seemed anxious to get a first glimpse of their new home. It was January, 1958.

Mary Harmon spotted the billboard first.

"Welcome home, Bear and Mary Harmon," it read.

"Now that's a touch of hospitality," she said.

"Hell, Mary Harmon, I didn't exactly expect a lynch mob."

"But the sign didn't mention me," Mae Martin complained.

"And it didn't mention old Doc either," her brother pointed out. "And he's the greatest dog in the world."

Mary Harmon looked at her husband. She could read the expression on his face perfectly, but she went ahead and asked the question.

"So tell me, Coach. How does it feel to be back in Tuscaloosa?"

He smiled. "A lot like home. Like we'll be here for a long while."

"Until death do us part," she said quietly.

They were making the turn onto University Boulevard. The Union Building was just ahead on the right, the quad stretched off to the left toward the soaring steps of the library building. The stately president's mansion was farther ahead on their right. Paul Jr. leaned forward, near his father.

"Papa, you don't seem as nervous here as you did in Texas."

"No, son. I'm not nervous. This time, I'm scared."

He made a right at the Union Building and kept driving. The football stadium came into view.

"Why are you scared?"

"Because we're starting from scratch all over again. But this time, the expectations are sky high. And son of a gun, I've never wanted to win as badly or work as hard as I do for this school. Because it's my school."

The office was shabby, the desk old, but the company in the room was good. Paul Bryant sat behind the scruffy desk, smoking a cigarette. Across from him, in a wobbly office chair, sat Coach Hank Crisp, the one-handed coach who had convinced Bear to play a game against Tennessee on a broken leg. Seated on an unopened packing crate next to him was a young assistant coach named Jerry Claiborne.

Bryant blew smoke toward the ceiling.

"Coach Hank, I don't know if we're wiser or just older," he said.

"I don't know either, Bear. But it sure is good to have old number 34 back home," Crisp said with a grin. "And it'll be even better now that we've got some decent recruits for you to work with."

"I know it had to be a scramble for you. Hell, by the time we got the deal done, recruiting was just about over. And I'm starting to think the NCAA ought to do away with it altogether. Just let the boy decide where he wants to go to school on his own without us having to go see him a dozen times. Of course, the alumni and the boosters would never hear of that." He considered the remainder of his cigarette for a moment and then elected to light a new one. "But we've got to push forward with whatever guys we've got here...the good and the bad. And I'm betting you and Jerry got more of the former than the latter."

"Claiborne knows more about that than I do."

"I don't know about the ability, Coach Bryant," the assistant said. "But they're good kids...homegrown boys who are proud of this program. At least what it was at one time."

Coach Bryant lit the end of the Chesterfield and sucked it until the fire caught.

"Jerry, I can't imagine winning meaning any more to them than it did to you guys at Kentucky."

"Yeah, but they've got more tradition to build on than we ever had up there."

"He's right," Coach Crisp said. "This is not a dead program. It may be a bit stale, but it's got plenty of life left yet."

Bryant snorted.

"Losing to Auburn four years in a row? Getting shut out by Tennessee three years in a row? Well, that's history. And I'm about to meet some eager young football players who are gonna change all that."

"If you crack the whip," Coach Crisp said.

Bryant studied the embers on the end of the cigarette. His eyes narrowed with the smoke.

"I don't know, Coach Hank. Every squad is different. I'm thinking these players need more polishing than pushing right now. I'm not sure it's best for me to come on like a gorilla the first time they lay eyes on me." Then he winked at his old coach. "But in time, yeah, we'll work 'em until they drop. For now, though, I'm just going to put a spit shine on Crimson Tide pride."

It was to be expected from a bunch of high-spirited young football players – freshmen who had just reported to campus for the first time as college football players. Their first meeting was about to start in Friedman Hall, but they were talking, laughing and carrying on horseplay as they waited for the coaches to show up. All of a sudden, one of them, a quarterback named Pat Trammell, jumped from his seat and stepped to the front of the room, taking a spot behind the big wooden school desk. He hollered and whistled, and the room quickly grew quieter.

"Hey, listen up! Shut up and listen to what I've got to say." The last of the horseplay stopped, and a hush fell over the big room. "How many of you are quarterbacks?" A half dozen players raised their hands. .

Tommy Brooker, who had been sitting next to Trammell, volunteered, "Oliver here is a quarterback." He pointed toward Bill "Brother" Oliver, whom he had played against in high school.

Trammell quickly sized up Oliver and the rest of them, then suddenly whipped out a formidable-looking switchblade knife from his pocket, opened the thing and began waving it slowly in front of him so the light from the overhead fixtures glinted dangerously off the shiny, steel blade. "You're all wrong. I'm the damn quarterback here, and every one of you needs to know it."

With that, Trammell threw the knife hard into the top of the wooden school desk. It stuck there, vibrating ominously from the force of the throw.

Some of the players squirmed a bit in their seats, but nobody disputed Trammell's pronouncement. ("Brother" Oliver would later say,

"There was no doubt who the leader of that team would be – not then and not for the next four years.")

Meanwhile, none of the freshmen players had noticed their head coach standing just outside the door, listening to what was going on. His quizzical look had already changed into a big grin.

Pat Trammell was his kind of player. Even if he was a quarterback.

Bear stepped into the room to greet his first Alabama recruits.

It was familiar territory for him: a room full of eager players, anxious to meet their new coach, wondering if he would live up to his billing – if he was really as tough as they had heard.

Bear walked the length of the room and stood in front of the assemblage. The whispers and scrapes of chairs died down to silence, as all eyes were on their new leader.

"Gentlemen, I just put up a sign in the football office that says, 'Winning isn't everything, but it beats anything that comes in second.' I want you to think about that. And not just when you're on the practice field or in a game." There were several puzzled looks. What was he saying? "You see, I want you to dress like winners. I want you to study like winners. I want you to have respect for others – yes, even those on the other side of the ball – like winners. And that includes respect for your mamas and papas, who are the reason you're here today. So tonight, I want you to write home and thank them for giving you the chance to play football for the University of Alabama."

Every eye was on Bear Bryant now. They had never heard a coach talk like this before. He slowly paced the front of the room as he went on.

"Believe me when I tell you this. Winning is contagious. If ol' Bobby acts like a winner, little Scooter there will, too. And on and on it will go until we don't have anything else on the team but winners. Now, I'm not about to bring up all the losing that's been going on around here lately. That's over. It's time to win now, and the Crimson Tide is gonna do that a lot from here on out. And we're gonna do it while displaying class in all areas. Now, let's get our minds on a very special sport, the game of football. And let's get ready to work our tails off for that national championship that we're gonna win much quicker than most folks think we will."

With that, the coach strode down the aisle in the middle of the room and out the door. No one moved. The coach had not ranted and raved. He had not ripped off his jacket and stomped on it. He had just told them flat out that they would be on a national championship team.

Almost as one, the group of players stood and cheered and clapped each other on the backs.

They had heard. And, for the moment, they believed.

A few minutes later, at a pay phone in the hallway outside the meeting room, Pat Trammell was talking to his mother.

"Mama, I've never heard anything like that. He told us to write home, but I got so excited I had to call instead." He listened for a moment. "I know it'll get harder. It's just that he's talking about a national title, and Alabama hasn't won but four games in the last three years. And Mama, I think every dang one of us believed what he said!"

Paul Bryant watched the practice from a high tower at one end of the field. From there, he could observe every drill for every position and miss very little of what was going on down there in his kingdom.

He blew the whistle, signaling the end of one segment of practice, and yelled, "Move to the next drill. And I mean double-time it! Hurry! We got plenty to do."

Players ran full speed from one part of the field to another. All except one. A big tackle who walked nonchalantly toward where the other linemen were already gathered, waiting for their position coach to tell them what he wanted them to do.

Bryant didn't miss the meandering player. He grabbed his bull-horn and pulled the trigger.

"I want everybody running!"

The lineman ignored the warning and made his own pace toward the drill position.

Bryant threw down the bullhorn and hit the ladder. In no time, he was on the ground and running toward the slow-moving player. When the player realized the coach was off the tower and beside him, he suddenly turned and trotted toward his group.

"Damn you, Williams! Freeze! Wait right there!"

The player kept jogging toward where he was supposed to be.

"I said stop, son, and that's what I mean for you to do."

Bryant grabbed the big player by the jersey and turned him around to face him.

"What did I tell you to do?"

The player shrugged and meekly said, "Run?"

"Then why the hell didn't you run?"

The player shrugged his shoulders again.

"You are a fat-ass loser. That's all you are. And it's losers like you that have caused Alabama to fall on such hard times lately."

"Sorry," the big lineman said sarcastically.

Coach Bryant grabbed more jersey, spun the big man around, and then kicked him hard in the butt.

"Sorry, hell! Get your ass moving toward that gate. I don't want to see you on this practice field again." But the player didn't move.

He half-turned back toward the coach, as if he might want to plead his case. But just then, Bryant slapped him hard on the side of his helmet and gave him a mighty shove. "You're fired, Williams. A fat slob like you makes me want to puke. You're finished, and Alabama will be that much the better for it."

By then, the player was running for the gate. Coach Bryant stood there, hands on his hips, and watched him leave. Every player and coach on the field had watched the whole episode play out.

"Now, I think I said something about the next drill."

And with that, he climbed back up the ladder to his lofty perch.

Chapter Nine:

Restoring Tide Pride

The surprise was obvious in the voices of the two sportscasters who were broadcasting the game on the radio. Even a casual listener could also sense the excitement in the roar of the crowd.

"Pinch yourself, Alabama fans. You are not dreaming!" the play-by-play announcer was saying. "My goodness! It's the Crimson Tide 10, Auburn nothing."

The color commentator picked up the recap with, "First, little Scooter Dyess...all 140 pounds of him...catches a TD pass. Then, Tommy Brooker kicks a field goal to put the Tide ahead for good."

"It's true, Big Red faithful," the play-by-play man assured his listeners, his voice cracking slightly with emotion. "And thus ends the misery at the hands of Auburn."

The color man lifted his microphone stand up, so he could rise and dance around the announce booth.

"This man is a magician! In two years, Paul William Bryant has put life into another dead football program. And now it's on to the Liberty Bowl for the 7-1-2 Alabama Crimson Tide."

Early the next Monday morning, Coach Bryant was already at work in his office, taking care of a

few last items before he began planning for the bowl game. But his concentration was broken by someone bellowing, "Roll Tide! Roll Tide!" outside his door. But Bear grinned when Red Blount burst through the door, continuing his chant. He leaned back in his chair and shook his head.

"Red, isn't this a little early for you to be tapping the keg?"

"Early? What is it? 6:30? Shoot, ain't nobody from Alabama slept in two nights now."

Bear reached for the telephone on his desk and began dialing a number.

"Well, you've got to excuse me while I call down to Auburn. I've got a few things to work out with Coach Jordan."

Blount sat down in one of the chairs across the desk from Bryant.

"Rub it in, Paul. And be sure to thank him for saying that you've changed the way football is played in the Southeastern Conference."

"Let's show some class, pal," Bear said as he listened to the ring. No one picked up so he flipped through his book to find another number.

"Bear, I'll be honest. I thought you were a fool last year when you quick-kicked five times out of our first nine plays against State. I figured we had hired ourselves a fool of..."

"We were banking on our defense."

"I know. And we won the game. But now we've got the whole package, and I figure..."

Bear held up his hand. Someone had finally answered the phone down at Auburn.

"Coach Jordan, please," he said and then scowled. "Nobody's in this early? Well, who is this? Well, Miss Cleaning Lady, what time do you expect Coach Jordan to arrive?" Bear winked at Blount. "You say nine o'clock? Well, sugar, this is Paul Bryant at Alabama. And I'm damned pleased to learn that you folks over there at Auburn don't take your football very seriously!"

The line of players making their way from the field and into the locker room were clearly dejected. To make matters worse, the public address announcer summed up the whole story for them to all hear again.

"And that's the end of the first half. It's Georgia Tech 15, Alabama zero."

Lee Roy Jordan, a center and linebacker, eased up behind quarterback Pat Trammell.

"We're about to get our tails chewed up one side and down the other," he said.

Trammell nodded. "We deserve it. One first down in two quarters."

But as the players sat around the locker room and girded themselves for the tongue lashing they knew was coming, their coach merely paced back and forth the length of the room, rubbing his chin, seemingly in deep thought. Finally, when he did talk, his voice was calm.

"Managers, please get these hard-working men some Cokes. And I'm asking you gentlemen to accept my apology for the lousy job of coaching that I've done today."

The players looked at him and then at each other. If this was a hide-tanning speech, it wasn't like any other they had ever heard before. Bear Bryant stopped pacing and stood there in the middle of the lot of them.

"And I've done an even sorrier job of getting you ready for what you're up against out there today. So I'm asking you to go out there and show some class in the second half. To bail me out. To make up for the sorry job I've done. I don't doubt that you can do it...maybe in the fourth quarter…but not because of me. Because of the type of mamas and papas you've got, and the kind of young men they sent to Alabama."

He headed for the door then but paused and turned around.

"That's all I ask. Just go out there and play with class and pride."

Then he left and shut the door behind him.

Later, the radio broadcast team described the waning moments of the game, straining to be heard over the thundering roar of the crowd.

"Even if we don't finish it off, Alabama has made a whale of a comeback," the play-by-play man was hoarsely reporting. "Down 15 to nothing with seven minutes to play, the Crimson Tide now trails 15 to 13 and drops back to receive a punt from the Yellow Jackets."

"It still looks gloomy," the color man said, but he had his fingers crossed anyway as he talked, just in case that might help the situation. "Only seconds left, and Alabama is down to its last timeout."

"There's only enough time for one…maybe two passes…then a field goal attempt."

"Yes, but remember, Tommy Brooker is hurt. That means Digger O'Dell, who has never attempted a field goal in a game, might become the man of the hour."

Down on the sideline, Bear Bryant seemed unaware that the clock was now down to double digits, or that his best chance to win the contest was out of the game, hurting.

"All right! All right! Fourth quarter! Fourth quarter!" he sang, clapping his hands and watching the eyes of his players for any sign of give-up. "Now we got ourselves a game. Now we've got a chance."

The public address announcer summed up the Tide's desperate situation.

"Alabama has a first down. Fourteen seconds left in the game."

Bear turned to an assistant.

"Let's see if we can get it to Wilson up the sideline. That's been open a few times already today. And tell him he better call time out if he doesn't score. Skelton will put the ball on the money. If he doesn't, we'll have a new quarterback next week."

Bear turned toward the bench as three or four whiskey bottles landed nearby. He ignored the missiles and yelled to no one in particular, "Where in hell is O'Dell? Get Digger up here with his kicking tee, and let's get the field goal unit ready." The coach finally noticed the whiskey bottles. "And somebody see if we can get a police officer to arrest some of these sons of bitches."

Meanwhile, out on the field, the pass play was already unfolding. Bobby Skelton, the quarterback, dropped back and flung the ball downfield to his target. Somehow, the receiver managed to stay in bounds and was finally brought down by Tech defenders a dozen yards short of the goal line.

"Stop the clock! Stop the clock!" Bear Bryant and several thousand Alabama faithful screamed in unison. The receiver managed to burrow out of the pile-up and give the "T" signal so one of the officials could see it.

Then a calm seemed to come over the coach. He took a glance at the scoreboard and another at the ball, resting on the green grass of Grant Field.

"First down Alabama at the 12 yard line," the PA declared. "Time out with three seconds left to play."

"Okay. Okay. It's our game to win now," Bear was saying. Then he spotted his raw, young kicker, Digger O'Dell, about to trot out onto the field. He grabbed the player and pulled him close.

"Hey, Digger," he said. "Don't be in a hurry. Just wait with me here for a few more seconds. Then just go out there and kick the ball through the uprights like you always do."

O'Dell gave him an odd look.

"But Coach, I've never tried a field goal in a game before."

Bryant slapped him on his shoulder pads and flashed him a broad grin.

"Hell, son, it's a piece of cake. Just take a deep breath and put your toe into it…just like you do in practice." Then he pulled the kid even closer. "You know I wouldn't send you out there if I didn't think you had enough guts to handle it." O'Dell nodded, but his eyes were still wide. "Then go out there and win the game for us and make everybody back home proud of you."

Richard "Digger" O'Dell trotted out toward where the rest of the team had been huddling.

The official blew the ball into play.

The differences between a losing locker room and a victorious one are mammoth. One is quiet, somber and painful to behold. The other is chaotic, loud and delirious.

The winning locker room that day was even more loud and chaotic than most. Players, mostly naked and bloody and sweating, whooped and screamed and pounded each other on the back. In a far corner, an improbable hero held court for the press when he could get a word in between the congratulations from his teammates. But the mob around the young kicker parted when Bear Bryant walked over to shake his hand.

"Digger, that was the damndest field goal I've ever seen. It looked like some bush league pitcher's knuckle ball."

"Coach, I swear it didn't clear the crossbar by more than two inches."

"I know, partner, but the score tells me your family and friends are just as proud of you now as I am."

"I hope so."

"And you know what else, son? They ought to build a statue to your honor back in Lincoln because, if I'm not wrong, we just showed everybody that Bama football is back on top to stay."

Chapter Ten:

National Power

There was something different about the young player Paul Bryant was showing around the campus. He was a handsome kid, but his dark, curly hair was long. Longer than anyone else passing them on the sidewalk that ran alongside the quad. His accent was sharp, too – not slow and drawling, like most of the other students around them. And he had a certain self-assurance about him. He was definitely different.

"Yep, Joe, we're coming on strong…and having you might be the last ingredient we need to become a true national power," Bear was telling the tall, lanky young man.

"Not might, Coach Bryant."

"Huh?"

"Not might. I am what you need."

Bear looked at the brash young northerner, a slight scowl on his face. He was no fan of cockiness.

"Look, Coach, I know I can play football," Joe Namath said with a pleasant grin. Bryant smiled back. It was hard not to like this youngster, even as he slowed his amble to study a pair of co-eds who happened to be walking past.

"I'm all for confidence, Joe," the coach said. "I just won't stand for..."

"How come you don't have any black players?" Namath interrupted to ask him.

"You don't miss much, do you?"

"No, sir. I can read, Coach. I know you had to get the okay of the Alabama state legislature so you guys could play against black players in the Liberty Bowl."

"The important thing there is that the lawmakers did clear it. And things will change here in time, Joe."

"Promise?"

"I don't make promises. I just do my best." The coach paused for a beat then went on. "And I appreciate the fact that you didn't ask for money to come down here and play for Alabama."

"Coach Bryant, I came to Alabama because I'm as honest as I am sure of myself. And I promise you that I'll work hard. That's one thing I learned in Beaver Falls...sort of like you did in Arkansas."

Bryant smiled.

"Joe, I'm betting you will become one helluva quarterback. And I think you have what it takes to be a leader, too, if you decide you want to be. If you can learn to take charge like Pat Trammell...with your natural athletic ability...you'll be a fine quarterback for the Crimson Tide, and you'll be able to make a mint someday, too, playing for money."

The bus driver could hardly tell if the engine had cranked or not. The load of Crimson Tide players were singing a spirited version of "Yea Alabama," the school fight song. The driver could tell from the gauges that the motor was running, so he engaged the clutch and the vehicle began rolling.

But then he felt a big hand on his shoulder. It was Bear Bryant, sitting in the seat behind him, next to Pat Trammell.

"Hold up a second, Mr. Driver." Bryant positioned himself in the aisle and motioned for his team to get quiet. "Gentlemen, I just want to personally thank you for this great victory today. I've had a helluva time beating Tennessee through the years, so giving them a 34-to-3 ass kicking is one of the sweetest victories ever." A big cheer rolled down the length of the bus. "And I also wanted you to know that everybody who stepped on that field this afternoon is going to be getting a ring as a memento of this win. I know you'll get it because I'm going to buy them!"

With another roar from his squad, Bryant nodded for the driver to get going. He started to sit down but then thought of something else. As they pulled away from the stadium, the coach waved for them to hush again.

"But let me remind you of something else, gentlemen. That damn ring will only be a reminder of what might have been if you don't beat hell out of everybody else left on our schedule!"

The huge banner behind the head table made clear the reason for the stellar gathering in the big banquet hall.

"WELCOME NATIONAL FOOTBALL FOUNDATION AND PRESIDENT KENNEDY," it read.

Several men stood conversing, getting ready to take their seats. They included Coach Bryant; Dr. Frank Rose, the school president; Benny Marshall, a sports columnist for The Birmingham News; Pat Trammell; sportscaster Mel Allen; and John Kennedy, the President of the United States. Secret Service men stood all about, as well as photographers and other invited guests. It was December of 1961, and it was a scene few Alabama fans could have pictured only a few years before.

"So, Dr. Rose," President Kennedy said. "Are we making any progress with integration down there at the University?"

"Slowly, Mr. President," Rose answered. "But as president of the school, I can assure you that it will happen in time."

Kennedy turned toward Trammell.

"I assume you agree, Mr. QB."

"I wouldn't know, sir. It's all hard to comprehend."

"It won't be easy, Mr. President," Coach Bryant said.

Kennedy took a sip of his cocktail and smiled.

"Yeah, about as easy as scoring touchdowns on your defense this season. How many points did your opponents get?"

"Twenty-two points all year. And we shut out the last five teams."

The President slowly shook his head, imagining such a thing.

"Then I guess you don't need much help from me in the Sugar Bowl."

"I appreciate the offer, Mr. President, but I expect you had better keep running the country."

A dark-clad Secret Service agent appeared from nowhere and stood next to Kennedy. "Mr. President, the students at Alabama are waiting to hear from you by telephone."

Kennedy said his goodbyes and began following the agent toward the phone hookup. He looked back over his shoulder.

"It's confidential, Coach Bryant, and still a year away, but I'm thinking about attending the Orange Bowl in Miami next year. Do you think you'll be there?"

The coach smiled crookedly.

"We'll do our best. And you do the same with those Russians."

Kennedy grinned back and walked on.

Chapter Eleven:

Hard-nosed Football

An angry Paul Bryant slammed the magazine down on his desk, sending sundry papers and envelopes flying in all directions. Benny Marshall of The Birmingham News and Charles Land from the Tuscaloosa News hardly flinched. They had been listening to Bear rage for the past fifteen minutes.

"What the hell is going on with you writers?" he demanded. "It's unreal what they are saying about us."

"Hold on, Coach, it's not us," Land said. "It's Furman Bisher in Atlanta and some of the others."

Benny Marshall leaned forward in his chair.

"Coach, you know you're going to get some of this now. You've gone twenty-one games without losing…so the guns are aimed at the biggest target."

Bryant picked up the magazine again. It was The Saturday Evening Post, a respected national publication. This time, he flung it across the room through the narrow gap between the two sportswriters.

"But this is war. Who gives them the right to say I'm a wild man? That I teach brutal foot-ball?"

"Oh, the U.S. Constitution," Marshall said. "It's called freedom of the press."

"And I suppose you believe in that crap...that they can print whatever they want to, even if it ain't true...and let every mama and papa in the nation read that the coach that wants to sign their boy to a football scholarship is nothing more than a barbaric son of a bitch."

"I didn't say they were right. Just that they have rights."

"I oughta sue their butts off. Hell, we're in the process of building something special here, and they're doing all they can do to tear it down." He leaned back in his big chair and took a deep draw of smoke from his cigarette. "Gentlemen, I don't teach kids to play dirty. I teach hard-nosed football. And I don't like some sports columnist in Atlanta taking something away from our little, bitty players just because they have big hearts and will go to the wall for their teammates and their school."

"I'll buy that," Land said.

"Then why don't you two fellas come to our defense? If you believe what I'm saying, write the damn truth and let your voices be heard."

Benny Marshall shrugged his shoulders. "You got it."

The coach leaned forward again, elbows on his desk and his eyes squinting through the cigarette smoke.

"In the meantime, I tell you what I'm going to do. I'm going to look for a way to put that damn magazine out of business."

Bear paced back and forth, his team waiting for his final words before sending them back onto the stadium floor. They could hear the constant rumble of the crowd, the dueling bands and the pre-game ceremonies, as the Orange Bowl drew closer to kickoff.

Bear had been true to his word. He had done all it took to get his team to Miami. So had the President of the United States. Mr. Kennedy would spend one half on the Alabama side of the stadium and the other half on the Oklahoma side.

But something was clearly bothering Bear. He finally stopped pacing, stomped out the stub of a cigarette he had just finished smoking and slid his hound's tooth hat back just a bit on his head so he could look into the faces of his squad.

The dressing room was already quiet. The team was considering what they needed to do this night to beat a fine Oklahoma Sooner team…and waiting for their coach's pre-game speech.

"Men, I've got to tell you. I don't like what I've seen for the last two months. You're pussyfooting around. You're not striking people the way you know how. That kind of football got you beat by one point against Tech. One damn point! That's all that kept you from being the national champs for a second straight year."

He surveyed the room. All the eyes – players, coaches, training staff – were on him.

"Look, I don't hold you totally responsible. I know you've been under study ever since that magazine article. But dammit, you can't let those bastards keep you from playing the way you know how."

There was no mistaking the look on his team's faces. They were mad. Number 54, Lee Roy Jordan, was pounding his right thigh rhythmically, ready to hit someone that very minute.

"Here's what I want you to do. I want you to go out yonder and knock every Sooner you see on his ass. But I want you to do it with class. I want you to knock the snot out of their noses, then I want you to reach down, help 'em up, then knock 'em down again!"

The room would have exploded then, except a game official had come in and was standing behind Bear.

"Coach Bryant," he said. "President Kennedy is on the field, so we need your captains right now."

Bryant nodded and looked toward number 54.

"Lee Roy, show some style…even if Kennedy did say he was pulling for Oklahoma."

"Yes, sir. We all will."

But the look in Jordan's eye was fearsome.

"What the hell is going on out there?" Bear screamed at the nearest assistant coach. "How many personal foul penalties are they going to call on us in one half of football?"

"We'll have to talk with Lee Roy," the coach responded. "The coaches up in the box say they can't see a thing we are doing wrong."

Just then, an official signaled for a time out, and Lee Roy Jordan ran full speed for the sideline where his coach was waiting.

"Coach, you've got to do something," he said with palms upraised in obvious frustration.

"No, dammit! You've got to quit that late hitting."

"That's not why they're flagging us, Coach. It's our signals. You know, when we holler 'Digger! Digger!' to let O'Dell know they're going to run his way? That stupid official thinks we're hollering 'Nigger! Nigger!'"

"Well, hell."

Bryant suddenly broke away and went running toward a startled game official out on the field. He shoved his face right up next to the official's and shouted to be heard over the crowd, which was taking great pleasure in his sprint onto the field.

"Dammit, listen to me. Go tell that deaf referee we are not screaming at that black boy. We're saying 'Digger,' dammit!"

The official looked thunderstruck.

"You're kidding me."

"Hell if I am. And I'm not letting you yellow-flag us out of a win."

"I'll pass the word, Coach. But I'll tell you this, too. There's no way those Sooners will beat your boys. Not the way they're rippin' and snortin' this afternoon."

Bear allowed himself the slightest of grins as he ambled back toward the sideline.

He was sprawled across a folding chair, sipping on a bottle of Coca Cola, holding court for several dozen reporters. They waited patiently for his pronouncement on how the game had gone.

"Obviously, it goes without saying that we are happy with the win. In fact, I would have been pleased with a one-point difference."

A reporter called out, "So, 17 to nothing surprised you?"

"Hell, yes it did. But when you've got Lee Roy Jordan on your side, a shutout is always possible. If they stay between the sidelines, ol' Lee Roy will get 'em."

"Coach, has Namath been that sharp all season?"

"Except against Georgia Tech. We all looked frail that day, and I was more sick than anybody else." The newsmen laughed. "But to answer your question, yeah, Joe is special. And if I don't screw him up, he'll be all-world before he's finished here. And fellas, that means Alabama ain't gonna be bad for a while."

"Then we'll write that you are on the verge of another national championship."

"I'm not foolish enough to make predictions like that. But I will tell you that life in Tuscaloosa isn't far short of a bed of roses these days."

With that, he leaned back, downed the last of the Coke, and then got up to join his team on the way to the bus.

She watched him, sitting there in the chair beside their bed. He was agitated, sweating, as he read and re-read the same article in the newspaper over and over again. He sucked hard on his cigarette and took sips of the whiskey and water in his glass, but he clearly didn't taste either one of them.

Mary Harmon checked the clock on the nightstand. It was 3:40 in the morning.

"Don't you know what time it is, sleepy head?" she asked him.

"Almost four," he answered without even checking the clock.

"I love you, Paul. Everybody does...the fans, the Alabama family." He didn't seem to hear her. His lips moved as he read the article under his breath again. "Have you slept at all?"

"Huh? No. I can't sleep. And I doubt those sons of bitches at The Saturday Evening Post can either."

She threw back the covers and crawled from bed.

"I'll go fix some breakfast. The eggs will be a lot better for you than that whiskey."

Bryant took another slug of the whiskey and slammed down the glass. He leapt from the chair, exploding, pacing, ranting all the while.

"The story of a college football fix! Alabama over Georgia! Bryant and Butts trading game secrets! Those sorry bastards! We could've beat that Georgia team by a hundred points if we had wanted to. Why is that damn writer so hell-bent on destroying what we're building?"

Mary Harmon paused at the door.

"Maybe he just doesn't like a team that wins so much."

He stopped pacing at the foot of their bed and seemed to notice her standing there for the first time. He lowered his voice.

"That's the point, Mary Harmon. I'm teaching kids how to win playing fairly, and then those boys have to read all this stuff they're saying about them. It's not me I'm worried about. It's the players. And that's the very reason Wally and I are going to sue the living crap out of that trash magazine."

He finally eased down to take a seat on the edge of the bed. She sat beside him and patted his knee as he went on. "I know what it is, Mary Harmon. It's my reputation as a driver. There was that thing with Darwin Holt and that Tech player and all the stuff they wrote about how brutal I am as a coach. Now they have to go and make up stuff like this to try to get at me. But Mary Harmon, I'm not about to change my methods just to avoid heartache like this. I'll take the heartache every time. I just hate it that they're hurting the players on both teams, saying the game was fixed – just like they hurt Darwin Holt with all the lies they wrote about that. And that's the reason I'm not going to let them get away with it!"

"That's the spirit, Paul. Now you're set to deal with it, just like a tough opponent on the football field. Go public. Let the people of Alabama and the whole country know the truth."

He looked at her and returned her sweet smile.

"That's exactly what I'm going to do. Now, did I hear you say something about some eggs?"

The television lights were hot, and he was sweating. He looked tired, too. But his voice was strong, and his eyes were steel hard as he talked.

"So I'm telling you, the people of Alabama and the nation, that Wally Butts and I did not contrive to fix a football game, as The Saturday Evening Post said. I've taken and passed a polygraph test...and I haven't seen the writer take one."

Back in Tuscaloosa, in the athletic dormitory, the players were gathered around the television set, watching and listening to their coach. Joe Namath and all-star center Gaylon McCollough were up front. McCollough reached and turned the volume on the TV set higher.

"But what bothers me most about this," Bear was saying, "Is that I've got players in Tuscaloosa…good young men, winners…who are on trial as much as me in this thing. That's not fair, and it makes me mad as hell. So don't believe what you read. Instead, applaud those young men from Alabama…and Georgia…who have paid the price to become winners."

With that, the show went to a commercial, and the players began to drift out of the room. Joe Namath didn't even look at his teammate when he said, "Gaylon, that's one helluva man."

"Uh huh. The kind of man you'd run through a brick wall for."

"He'll beat this thing," Namath said. "Just like he does everybody we play."

The star quarterback sat with his head down, considering the pattern in the carpet. His coach sat across the desk from him, trying to find a comfortable position in his old office chair.

"Okay, get your head up, son, and give it to me straight," the coach finally said.

Joe Namath swallowed hard and looked Bear in the eye.

"It's true what you heard. I've let you down, Coach. I drank too much."

"No, Joe. You didn't just let me down. You let your teammates down, too."

"I know."

"And you're going to pay for it. You're not going to the Sugar Bowl with us."

Namath's head dropped again.

"Yes, sir. I figured that."

"Is that fair?"

"Yes, sir. And I'm sorry. You've had a bad enough year because of that damn magazine."

Bryant leaned forward and crossed his arms on the desk.

"I know there were others with you. You want to tell me who they were?"

"No, sir. I've let down my teammates enough without getting anyone else into trouble."

Bryant studied his player's face for a moment.

"Discipline, Joe. That's all you need to be great. But that can't come from me. It's got to come from within you."

"Yes, sir. Those other guys will get us a win over Ole Miss without me."

"Maybe."

Namath stood and shook his coach's hand.

"Next year, Coach Bryant, I won't let you – or anybody – down."

Chapter Twelve:

Closing the Gap

The room was clouded with smoke. The half dozen men gathered around the poker table stared intently at the fan of cards each held in his hands.

"That's ten to you, Coach," one man said through his cigar.

"I'll need another marker," Bryant growled.

"No way, Coach," one of the other players protested. "I think that's enough for you tonight."

"Damn right," another sang out. "Enough of us and enough of that juice."

"Hell, you boys know I'm good for the cash." He checked the corners of the cards in his hand. "And besides, I'm sittin' here with three smiling ladies."

"Bear, it ain't your bank account that bothers us. It's your memory."

"What does that mean?"

"You get amnesia when it comes to poker debts. Especially when you been drinking."

"And don't forget," someone across the table said. "Fall practice starts in a few days."

"That's right," another man added. "A man can't defend a national championship hung over, so maybe you ought to...

Bryant interrupted with a laugh.

"He damn sure can if he has Sloan and Stabler under center. If you think Namath was something taking us to number one, wait until you see that duo."

"Yeah, but remember, Bear, ain't neither one of 'em ever tried to throw the ball between them hedges at Georgia."

"Or been in Baton Rouge with all them crazy Cajuns on a Saturday night," another added.

Bryant snorted and threw his cards face down on the table.

"Well, you boys can go to hell. And as for me, I'm going home."

The poker players watched him don his hound's tooth hat and coat and leave. One of them flipped over his cards.

No queens. Three threes.

"He's as good a bluffer as he is a football coach!"

State Trooper Joe Smelley worked hard to shove a few raucous Tennessee fans out of Bear Bryant's path, as he made his way toward the Legion Field dressing room. The coach followed the officer closely, paying no attention to the jeers and jibes from the orange-clad devotees of the Vols who leaned over the fence to taunt him.

He didn't have the heart to look up at the massive scoreboard again. He knew all too well what it said.

"Alabama 7, Tennessee 7."

He continued to replay the final drive in his mind. His quarter-back, confused about the downs as they drove for a sure win, had just thrown the ball out of bounds to stop the clock, even though it was fourth down.

When they got to the entrance of the dressing room, he found his team still standing outside, milling around the closed door.

"Get your asses in there," he ordered. "Anybody gets beat by Georgia and tied by Tennessee oughta be too ashamed to be seen in public."

"It's locked, Coach," a player said.

"Well, hell," the coach said. "Captain Smelley, would you please get out your gun and shoot the damn lock off that door?"

The Trooper only considered the order for an instant.

"I can't, Coach. That would be too dangerous."

"Manager!" Bryant yelled, but there was not one in sight. "Manager!" he yelled again in his booming bass voice.

Jim Goosetree, the trainer, eased up next to Bryant.

"They're still out there on the field gathering up all the gear, Coach," he said.

"Then ya'll get out of my way."

The coach stepped back a few feet, lowered his shoulder and ran full speed into the locked door. The force of the blow tore the door off its hinges and sent it crashing into the locker room.

Bryant picked up his hat, stood up straight and walked inside, as if nothing was amiss.

His team humbly followed him in.

A Birmingham police officer came along momentarily and spotted the damage.

"Who did this?" he inquired.

"Coach Bryant," someone answered.

The policeman merely shrugged and walked on.

"Thank the Lord it's the last day of 1965, because it has been one helluva year for us."

The players, assembled in the meeting room in front of him and all adorned in their practice sweat suits, nodded in agreement. Bryant went on.

"But a lot has happened since the loss at Georgia and the tie with Tennessee. Now, it's show time. The Orange Bowl tomorrow night. The start of a new year. Plus, new life for the defense of our national championship."

Several of the players looked at each other, puzzled expressions on their faces. There was no way they had a shot at the national championship. Not with a loss and a tie. Not with Michigan State, Arkansas and Nebraska ahead of them in the polls. Even if they could knock off Nebraska the next day, there was no way they could win the national title.

Bear turned and walked purposefully to the chalkboard behind him and began writing in big letters.

"#2 Arkansas loses in the Cotton Bowl to LSU."

He turned and made sure everyone was watching, reading the words, then lifted the chalk again.

"#1 Michigan State loses in the Rose Bowl to UCLA."

Again, he turned to see that all the squad was reading along.

"#4 Alabama beats the hell out of #3 Nebraska...Alabama is National Champion."

The team hummed as they considered the equations on the chalkboard.

"I've always told you gentlemen to expect the unexpected...to stick to your knitting...and to keep the faith. Well, dammit, now is a good time to do it!"

Fists were in the air and cheers cascaded across the room before the last words were out of the coach's mouth.

Twenty-four hours later, the cheers came from the Alabama rooting section as the final seconds of the Orange Bowl faded away beneath the Miami moon. Everything Bear had written on that chalkboard had come to pass. The Tide had beaten Nebraska 39 to 28 and were national champions.

Once again, all was right with the football world.

Dr. Pat Trammell slumped tiredly in his office chair, using his shoulder to keep the telephone to his ear. He had not even taken the time to get out of his surgical scrubs. He had to make the call to his old coach first.

The young physician had plenty on his mind. Football was the first thing.

"Coach, I wish I was there with you this week. There's nothing more fun than getting ready to beat Auburn's ass...no matter how many times we've done it before."

Trammell could hear the smile in his former coach's voice.

"You got that right, Pat. I wish I was certain we'll do it to 'em again this year, but this isn't one of our better teams. I can't quite get a read on these boys."

"Come on, Coach, we've still got a shot at the national title. Just like two years ago. We've got a loss and a tie, and if everyone in front of us loses again..."

Both men had a chuckle at that thought.

Then Trammell cleared his throat and swallowed hard. "Hey, Coach, that's not the only reason I'm calling. I...uh...have a little problem."

"I hope it's not any of your family."

"No, sir. It's me. See, I've got this weird kind of cancer. The doctors want to take a look at it. I'm going in to the hospital tomorrow."

"What? Cancer? Don't say that!"

"Hey, Coach. Don't get so shook up about it. Hell, it's probably just some little something. But...you know...it could be dangerous, which is why they want to check it out. And why I'd really appreciate it if I could see you if you have time."

"When are you going in?"

"Nine in the morning."

"I'll be there at seven."

When he hung up the phone, Paul Bryant leaned back in his chair and considered the ceiling, then rubbed his eyes. Tears were coming, and he didn't care.

"Pat Trammell is the toughest player I ever coached," he said softly to himself. "If he's scared, then there's something to be scared about."

A warm desert wind blew in from the west as the foursome of golfers prepared to tee off on the first hole. Fans cheered as they drew their drivers from their bags. One of them, Bob Hope, walked over and took a microphone from someone and smiled for the crowd and cameras.

"I was scared to death when they told me I was paired with Bear Bryant," the comedian said. "I thought, my God, I'm about to play golf with a man so ugly he once spooked the muzzle off a grizzly." The crowd laughed, while Bear Bryant stood there and grinned. "But I am honored to be playing with Bear today. He's the only coach in America who asks prospects what size national championship rings they wear while he's still recruiting them. And the only coach who actually got nominations for president at the Democratic National Convention. Bear's always been good at getting votes…except, of course, in '66."

At that, the coach raised an eyebrow and offered a slight smirk in the comedian's direction. Then the smirk turned into a broad smile, and he proudly stuck out his chest as he walked to the tee box. With the TV cameras on him, he gave a slight tip of his hound's tooth hat to Hope, then got set to hit the ball as far and as straight as he could.

The mood in the conference room was tense.

"Coach, we've lost that halfback from Miami Dade," an assistant coach hesitantly reported.

"To who?" Bear roared.

The young assistant swallowed before he answered, "To Auburn."

"That's ridiculous! We're beating the devil out of them. Eight out of the last nine."

"That's what they're selling. That he's the one that can turn it around."

"It might help if you visited him, Coach."

"Hell, I don't have time for that. I've got business meetings. And a damn fine grandson to visit."

The assistant took a deep breath and plowed on.

"Hell, Coach, Auburn and the others are closing the gap on us."

Bryant stood up and started for the door.

"Look, if you guys can't peddle the best college football program in America, then maybe I need to find some new recruiters."

The two men sat next to each other on the pier, their legs dangling over the edge. Paul Bryant held his grandson, Marc Tyson, in his lap, while he eyed the cork from his fishing line bobbing gently in the water. Paul Jr. watched his nephew squirm in grandpapa's lap. The child seemed to have little interest in this fishing stuff, but Bear was determined to show him how it was done.

"Now, we're getting a nibble. Here's how it's done, big fella. Just watch the cork and be still."

Marc squirmed some more, trying to get loose.

"Papa, I'm not sure Marc knows what you're saying."

"I'm not sure I do either. I thought there was supposed to be some..." He suddenly gave the pole a yank as the sinker disappeared from the surface. He lifted the hook out of the water. There was a smallish bream on the end of the line. He pulled it closer, so Paul Jr. could get the fish off the hook. "Oh, yeah! Here we go! Watch him, Marc. We got him, partner. Your first fish. You and I are gonna catch plenty more before you grow up."

Practice had gone well, and Bear was humming contentedly as he entered his office. He still had plenty of work to do…several hours' worth. Plays to diagram, meeting notes to go over, as they prepared for yet another bowl game.

He almost missed the telephone message someone had left on his chair. He felt the blood drain out of him when he read what was written on it.

"Pat Trammell near death. University Hospital."

He made the drive to Birmingham in record time. Soon, he was in his former QB's room, talking quietly with him. He couldn't believe how weak Trammell's voice was, how tired and fragile he looked. Pat feebly motioned toward an autographed football that sat in a place of honor on the windowsill.

"Coach, for you guys to give me that football was…"

"Whipping Auburn is special for every Alabama guy."

"It sure is for me. I'm an Alabama man through and through."

"I know, Pat. You're a big reason we've been whipping everybody lately." The coach leaned over and put his hand on top of Trammell's. "And Doctor Trammell, I love you because of all you did for the school."

The QB closed one eye and looked up at his coach.

"Okay, so do me one favor, Coach."

"Anything."

"Don't fill me up with all that sentimental crap. That's not me. People die every day. In my business, I've seen plenty of it." Bear smiled, winked and nodded, then waited for Trammell to finish coughing. "I don't know of anybody who has had it as good as I have. Remember, Coach, we've won a hell of a lot more than we've lost."

Bryant smiled and winked again, but this time he had to quickly turn his head.

The coach didn't want Pat Trammell to see the unexpected tears that suddenly broke loose and rolled down his cheeks.

It could have been a scene from any one of thousands of homes around Alabama on a fall Saturday: the family, gathered around the radio, listening to the Bama game. Some wearing red jerseys or Bama baseball caps.

But on this October Saturday in 1969, the families clustered around their radios wore grim expressions. The play-by-play man's words were not to be believed, but they were real…and painful.

"They are counting down the final seconds here in Nashville, and the Vanderbilt fans are ecstatic. The Commodores have defeated Alabama 14 to 10 in an upset that will shock the nation. Watson Brown, the crafty QB from Cookeville, Tennessee, was exactly as advertised by Coach Bryant all week. The Bear warned reporters that Brown was far better than your typical sophomore quarterback…"

But by that point, many of the radios had been snapped off as if, by merely shutting off the voice, it would all be rendered untrue.

Vanderbilt beating Alabama? The football world had somehow spun right off its axis.

Charley Thornton, the co-host of Bear Bryant's weekly Sunday wrap-up show had done his introduction already, recapped the previous day's game and turned it over to the coach to begin his own run through. But there was a long pause before Bear started talking.

When he finally did, he looked directly into the camera and spoke without hesitation, as if he had been rehearsing exactly what he planned to say to the people of Alabama that day.

"I know a lot of you are angry because Tennessee linebacker Steve Kiner said all the pride had gone out of the red Alabama jersey. Well, I'm not mad. He's right. When they beat us 41 to 14, then you can bet something is going wrong with our program."

Jim Murray, the highly respected sports columnist for the Los Angeles Times, had finished writing his story on the just-completed game and was packing up his typewriter. It was a long flight back to the West Coast, and he would be glad to leave behind the heat and humidity of central Alabama in September. He took one more swig of his soft drink and was about to head for the elevator when he noticed a young pup of a reporter approaching.

"Excuse me, Mr. Murray, but I've just started my career as a sportswriter. I'm a great admirer of your work. I was just wondering what you wrote about the game."

Murray considered the kid for a moment and decided to share the hook for the story he had just completed.

"Okay, I'll tell you if you'll hold that elevator door for me. Thanks. I wrote that Sam Cunningham, the great Southern Cal running back, in a 42-to-21 victory over the Crimson Tide, advanced the cause of integration in Alabama more in one night than Martin Luther King did in a decade."

Dr. David Matthews, the young-looking president of the University of Alabama, could not believe what he was reading on the piece of paper he held. He looked back across the desk at his head football coach, Paul Bryant, and at Jeff Coleman, the president of the Alabama Alumni Association.

Bear held his trademark hat in his hand, and there was a grim but determined look on his face.

"So, Mr. President, who do you think should replace me?" he asked.

"Nobody," Matthews replied immediately, without even thinking about the question. "Nobody, because I'm not accepting this resignation."

"You have to. I've lost the touch."

Coleman moved forward to the edge of his chair and said, "That's not what your record says. You've got 108 wins in thirteen years at Alabama."

Bryant fiddled with his hat.

"Yes, but only twelve in the last two years…and I've lost two in a row to Auburn and four straight games to Tennessee. That's a sorry record."

"It's just a down cycle," Matthews said. "We'll come back."

"Hell, Mr. President, I've put our school in a hole. And it's my fault because I got fat and lazy…spent more time playing golf and making money than I did coaching this team. I probably should have taken all that money the Miami Dolphins offered me, but I always swore I wouldn't leave Alabama for financial reasons. This is different, though. I want my school to have the best, and I'm not giving it the best right now."

Matthews studied his coach for a moment and asked, "So tell me, Paul, do you want to coach?"

"Sure, I do. But Alabama deserves much better than it's getting."

"Well, I'm president of this university, and it's my decision. And I disagree with you."

Coleman turned toward Bear.

"All right. Now that that's settled, Paul, I'd like to hear what we have next season."

"Frankly, we're short on players. We can't win passing the ball, so we'll have to try a new offense." Bryant grinned crookedly. "Oh, and your football coach plans to work as hard as he ever has."

Chapter Thirteen:

Revival

The jersey on the short, skinny quarterback was soaked through with perspiration. The August heat was oppressive, but the '71 Tide team had much work to do and a short time to do it. Terry Davis had just finished a full practice and was still holding tightly to a football as he headed for a cool shower and something to drink. He didn't slow down, not even when Coach Bryant fell into step beside him.

"Good practice, son. I think this just might work," Bear said.

"Yes, sir. I do, too," Davis said. "If we run this wishbone offense to perfection, we've got a good chance to beat Southern Cal."

"That's number one Southern Cal," Bear corrected.

Davis pounded the football against his thigh pad.

"It's get-even time, Coach. And if you'll accept the opinion of a skinny little quarterback, I don't think they'll be able to stop Johnny Musso."

Bear ignored the sweat and grass on the player's jersey. He put his arm around his quarterback.

"If that's the case, we'll win big again this season. And fans will remember Terry Davis as the quarterback that led the revival of the Crimson Tide."

It was much cooler in November, but the atmosphere at Birmingham's Legion Field was boiling hot. Undefeated Alabama against unbeaten Auburn. Heisman Trophy favorite Pat Sullivan, the quarterback from Auburn, against all-star running back Johnny Musso, "The Italian Stallion."

By the end of the game, there was little drama, though. Up in the press box, before the big "Alabama Radio Network" sign, the broadcast team could hardly control their glee.

"Well, folks, for Alabama, this has been a dream day," the play-by-play announcer was saying. "31 to 7, Crimson Tide."

"That's right, John. Alabama is back with a high-powered running offense, and Nebraska is waiting in the Orange Bowl in a game that will determine the number one team in the nation."

The revival was in full swing.

Familiar scene: a roomful of sports reporters…Bear Bryant, sitting on a folding chair, a Coke in one hand and a cigarette in the other.

But this night, the coach looked worn down, tired.

"You saw it for yourselves, so there's little I can add. Nebraska took us to the woodshed, like men playing with boys. But gentlemen, I won't let a 38-to-6 drubbing detract from this season. No matter what you might have seen out there tonight, the Tide is rolling again."

Another bowl, another press conference. This one on the eve of a classic showdown.

Bear surveyed the crowd of jaded sportswriters and smiled.

"Gentlemen, I've got goose bumps just thinking about it. For Notre Dame and Alabama to play for the first time in the Sugar Bowl with both teams unbeaten…well…it's college football at its finest."

One of the writers caught his eye, and Bryant nodded at him.

"Coach, you've already been named UPI national champ. Why would you want to...?"

Bryant held up his hand, stopping the reporter in mid-question.

"I don't give a damn about the polls. The real champion of college football will be decided right here in New Orleans."

Later, among friends, Bryant shared the real reason he had come to New Orleans to play Notre Dame, when he could have easily gone anywhere else, played a lesser team and protected his national championship. It was all for an old friend, Aruns Callery.

The two had been close for years. Callery had once used his influence on the Sugar Bowl committee to get the Tide an invitation in a season when the team was barely good enough to be there. And Bryant, who was always steadfastly loyal, was more than willing to help a friend in a tight spot.

Callery had been indicted in a gambling conspiracy case and was about to face trial. For that reason, he had fallen out of favor with other members of the bowl committee. Which is why Bryant agreed to bring his number one team down for a showdown with the Irish.

"The Sugar Bowl don't deserve it," he said. "But I'm doing it for Aruns."

The result was one of the most memorable college football games in history.

The stroll to the middle of the field for the after-the-game handshake was an especially long one this night. The words and numbers "Notre Dame 24, Alabama 23" glimmered at him from the scoreboard through the smoke of the post-game pyrotechnics.

He touched Captain Smelley, his Trooper bodyguard, on the arm.

"Captain Smelley, I think we just saw the best damn football game ever played. And frankly, right now, the only thing I could wish for is another shot at the Irish!"

It was a simple football play, not dissimilar to many others that were run that day at Birmingham's historic Legion Field Stadium. The visiting team's running back made a simple sweep to the right and was met by a wall of Bama defenders. The lick wasn't noticeably forceful, but when the play was whistled over, the running back for Texas Christian lay motionless. Kent Waldrep did not get to his feet and trot back to his team's huddle like everyone else did.

Waldrep's head had slammed against the artificial turf, resulting in a freak spinal cord injury. From that moment, he was paralyzed from the neck down. Doctors rushed onto the field and worked to keep the player breathing, while both teams clustered together, sadly hanging their heads. Some kneeled and prayed.

Finally, an ambulance rolled onto the field, and the young player was loaded aboard, bound for emergency care at University Hospital near downtown Birmingham. Along with players and coaches from the TCU team, Paul Bryant stood there next to the stretcher as it disappeared into the back of the ambulance and gave the injured player a word of encouragement.

The next day, after he had taped his regular Sunday television show, Bryant went directly to see the TCU player. Lying motionless in his hospital bed, Waldrep no longer had the appearance of a 20-year-old athlete.

"I'm real sorry, son," said Bear, his face showing the anguish. "I just feel awful. I wish there was something I could do for you."

"You've already done plenty for me, sir. It was a privilege to play against your team." The running back managed a smile. "It's not anyone's fault, coach. It's just football. Sometimes people get hurt."

"I know, son. I know. But I'll always be there if you ever you need me. Just know that I'm on your team."

(Bryant visited him regularly while he was in the Birmingham hospital, and he sat for hours with the family in the waiting room, sharing tears and trying to give them some kind of encouragement. For the rest of the coach's life, he regularly made time to write a note or place a phone call to Waldrep – a young man he had never met until that Saturday at Legion Field. At Bear's funeral, Kent Waldrep was one of the speakers.)

Paul Bryant was mad. Mad that his team had once again come up short against Notre Dame when everything was on the line. The 1975 Orange Bowl. The national championship. Everything.

And at the post-game press conference, he was ready to pounce when the first brave reporter began asking the inevitable question.

"Coach, that's two straight losses to Notre Dame. Do you...?"

"I'm aware of that," Bear snapped. "And I guess you're going to tell me next that we haven't won a bowl game since 1966."

"Well, now that you mentioned..."

"Let me tell you something, pal," the coach said, pointing the ember end of his cigarette at the scribe for emphasis. "In case you don't know, there's something special about making it to sixteen straight bowl games. And there's no shame in playing for number one in three of the last four." Bear watched the other reporters furiously scribbling notes, trying to capture his quote. "Let me ask you gentlemen, do you know of a program anywhere that can top that? Hell, no! And my heart goes out to those kids in the room there wearing red. Hell, they've lost by one point and by two points to damn good Notre Dame teams. And they might've won both of those games if their old coach had done his part."

"Like what?" one of the reporters asked.

Bryant scratched his jaw and took another swallow of his Coke.

"I don't know. Maybe stayed home and played checkers. But their day is coming. They're good kids, all of them. And if they keep knocking, that damn door is going to pop open for them one day."

His call to Aruns Callery of the Sugar Bowl committee had come out of the blue.

The committee had been trying to form an alliance with the Southeastern Conference, like the one the Orange and Rose Bowls had with other conferences. But the one person who would benefit the least from such a deal was Bryant. Most years, he could pick and choose, taking his team to the bowl of choice. Sometimes the Sugar didn't offer the best match up – or the most money – for the SEC champion.

The rest of the coaches and athletic directors in the SEC had refused to commit until Bear made his decision. It took him several months, but Bryant eventually blessed the idea.

"Aruns, I'm not thrilled about it," Bear Bryant growled into the telephone. "But I have to think about what's best for the conference, and it looks like you've got yourself a deal."

It's rare to capture two legends in a single snapshot, and the two fans in the hotel lobby were taking advantage of the opportunity. The man was directing, urging his wife, Bear Bryant and Ohio State head coach Woody Hayes to stand closer, so he could fit them all in the frame. The flash blinded all three, but they laughed about it.

It was New Orleans on New Year's Day, 1978, and a sizeable crowd was now gathering to get their own photos taken with two coaches.

"Coach Bryant, could I get you and Coach Hayes to shake hands for a shot?" one of them asked.

"What do you think, Woody?" Bear asked with a mock growl. "Would that blow our cover?"

"Well, Bear, my fans back in Columbus might not like it, but we can give it a try."

The fan thanked them again and gushed, "Now I can prove that I've been in the presence of the two greatest football coaches in history."

"Thank you, my friend, but that covers a lot of ground," Bryant laughed.

Hayes and Bryant shook hands with several of the other fans who had gathered there, then made their escape through a convenient exit.

"Well, Woodrow, I guess it's time to meet the press," Bryant said, as they made their way down the stairwell.

"We've got about fifteen minutes. Let's chat a while. Maybe I can pick your brain."

"That won't take long. I'm afraid it's slim pickings."

Hayes chuckled and said, "Your record the last several years says otherwise. Here you are at another bowl game. You just pick the one you want to go to…and you probably help the rest of the bowls choose their teams, too. I need to get on your list for next year, so you can get us into another good one."

"Aw, Woodrow, we just try to help out where we can. Try to use a little influence if it helps one of my 'boys' get a good bowl now and then."

"You're much too modest, Paul."

"Well, I've been lucky when…"

"No, sir, Paul. You've kept in step, changed with the times." They stopped on the stair landing on the floor where they were headed but stood there, talking. "Let's face it. We're the only two old codgers left in this game. And you're overwhelming folks, while I'm just lucky to get by."

"Woody, I've got good people working for me. Always have. And they're the ones who sweat. Oh, and some damn fine players, too. If I have any talent at all, it has been the ability to find the heart of a football team."

"But, Paul, the kids are changing. It just doesn't seem to mean as much to them anymore."

"That's true, Woody. But winning is still important to them. It's just that they've got so many other interests now."

Hayes shook his head and leaned against the railing.

"That's what I'm finding hard to accept."

"Partner, we just have to recognize that it's not a war to them. It's only a game that involves combat tactics…blocking and tackling with some strategy thrown in."

Woody Hayes held out his hands in exasperation.

"Damn, Paul, I just won't accept it."

"Then I'm afraid you're in for a lot more frustration." Bear's face split into a broad grin. "And I'm in favor of Alabama adding to it tomorrow night."

The two sportswriters stood in line at the bank of pay phones, waiting for their chance to call in their recap of the post-Sugar Bowl press conference with Bear Bryant.

"That Bear is one hell of a quote, ain't he?" one asked. "And he seems to be getting better as the years pass."

"Can you believe he was bragging on Woody, even after he beat him 35 to 6?"

"I think he went a little overboard, though. 'Woody is a great coach, and I'm not too bad.' Whatever you say, Bear."

The two reporters laughed as they slowly moved toward the phones.

Keith Jackson looked flushed. Frank Broyles was obviously about to hyperventilate. The ABC television cameras had zoomed in on the duo in the press box as they recapped the scene during a time out. The words at the bottom of the TV screen confirmed it was the Sugar Bowl...in the Superdome, New Orleans...New Year's Day, 1979.

Jackson was almost yelling to be heard over the captured bellow of the crowd inside the dome.

"Whoa, Nellie! It's coming down to one play that could be for all the spoils. Penn State and Alabama. One snap for the Nittany Lions, and one foot to go for the tie."

Broyles leaned into his microphone.

"You're so right, Keith. And it's incredible. Penn State, trailing 14 to 7 to the Crimson Tide, has taken one crack at the end zone from less than a yard away and come up short. Now comes their last try from a foot out."

Jackson had an opinion about the monumental play that was soon to be set loose on the floor of the Superdome by the waving official.

"It's old-fashioned stuff. Bryant and Paterno at the controls in the fourth quarter of the biggest of games."

Down where the TV cameras and the eyes of thousands of fans in the building were directed, Penn State quarterback Chuck Fusina took advantage of the time out and walked to the line of scrimmage to see precisely how far his team needed to go for a game-tying score.

A few yards away, the Alabama defenders in their crimson jerseys huddled in the end zone. One of them, tackle Marty Lyons, climbed up from one knee and ambled over to where Fusina seemed to be measuring the distance left – all the way down to the inch.

"How far is it?" Lyons asked him.

Fusina studied the space between the nose of the ball and the white stripe of the goal line a moment more.

"Ten inches," he replied.

Lyons looked him right in the eye and said, "You better pass."

Back up the field, on the Bama sideline, Bear Bryant was talking with an assistant coach.

"What do you think?" he asked.

"They're going to run right at us again," the assistant declared.

Bryant's jaw worked, as he considered the possibilities.

"Let's hope so."

The slam of bodies into bodies, the staccato grunts as vicious contact was initiated by the snap of the football, were all audible, even over the river-rapid roar of the frenzied crowd.

"They didn't make it!" Bryant yelped. "No way! No way! Son of a bitch, we've stopped 'em."

Sure enough, as a confirmation, the official was signaling first down back up the length of the field. The Tide had held on a classic goal line stand. Bama would soon be number one again.

Paul "Bear" Bryant's revival of his beloved team was now complete.

Chapter Fourteen:

Chasing Warner
and Stagg

The other patrons in the New Orleans oyster bar couldn't believe their luck. There was that football coach, Bear Bryant, leaned up against the bar, talking to two other men, eating raw oysters as fast as the crew behind the counter could shuck them, washing them down with cold beers. Still, the patrons held back from going up and asking for autographs. They could see he was engrossed in conversation with the two men.

One was Billy Varner, Bear's personal bodyguard. The other was Aruns Callery of the Sugar Bowl. It was late December of 1979, and the Tide was back in The Big Easy for yet another showdown at the Superdome.

"How about another beer, Bear?" the bartender asked.

"One more, Felix. Then I better quit." Coach Bryant looked toward Callery. "You know, Aruns, you folks have more press conferences than the President of the United States."

The bartender was back with the beer and spoke before Callery could respond.

"That's the Sugar Bowl, Bear. And they have to hype it even with number one Alabama back in town."

"Yes, sir, and I'm betting he makes it three straight wins," Callery said. "Holtz has Arkansas going good, but it's no match in my estimation."

One of the men shucking oysters behind the bar jumped in.

"There ain't nobody can handle the Big Red. Man! It's twenty wins in a row and growing."

Bryant chased an oyster with a big gulp of the cold beer.

"There's something the news media has missed that I'm damn proud of, too."

"What's that?" Callery asked.

"Win, lose or draw against Arkansas, we've won more games in a decade than any college football program in history. It's at 102 now with 103 coming soon, I hope."

The oyster shucker whooped.

"And to think you tried to quit!" the man said.

The bartender waved off the comment. "That was just a bluff...something to set the stage for a new start, wasn't it, Bear?"

"No, I was as serious as an executioner. Ready to go. And now I'm dreading the day when I will have to actually do it."

The oyster shucker laughed out loud. "Yeah, but you'll just move to the NFL when you quit, won't you?"

"I reckon not," Bear growled. "I had my chances on that already. The folks with the Atlanta franchise came to me back in '66. I told them I wouldn't ever move to the same town as Furman Bisher and that damn newspaper he works for. Hell, I pack a lunch bucket anytime I go over there, just to keep from spending money in that damn town. I also had a chance to buy into the New York Jets with Jimmy Hinton and some other friends, but Sonny Werblin told me to invest my money instead in the Miami Dolphins. I wish I had. They've done real well."

Bryant threw down another oyster and took a big swig of his beer.

"The last serious offer I had was from Joe Robbie back in '69. He wanted me to come down to coach the Dolphins. I agreed to go. We drew up a contract in a hotel room in Birmingham, and I all but told Mr. Robbie that I would take the job. I had Joe Namath come down to Tuscaloosa and go over the Dolphin roster with me, man for man, and even then he could tell that they were going to be real good in a year or two. Howard Schnellenberger...he played and coached for me...he told me the same thing Joe did, that I could win with that bunch left-handed. When I went to the school president, Dr. Matthews, and Red Blount from the Board of Directors, to tell them I was leaving, they didn't hem and haw. They told me if that was what I wanted to do, I should go on and take the job, just so long as I did one thing for them. I had to find them a replacement that was as good a coach as I was, but younger."

Bear winked broadly.

"Course, I couldn't find anybody as good as me, so I had to turn down Mr. Robbie and his kind offer to coach the Miami Dolphins."

All the men guffawed.

"Bear, you a mess!" the oyster shucker laughed. He slid another tray in front of his famous customer.

"Well, it's the truth," Bear said, as he gathered up another shellfish and slid it into his mouth. "Mr. Robbie and the Dolphins did all right for themselves, though. Better than if they had brought me down there. Don Shula turned out to be something special, I'd say." Bryant downed a big swallow of beer. "Hell, it's too late now to even be talking about such things."

"You got all kinds of time, Bear. Ten more good years for sure."

"Fella, I'm 66 years old and moving too quick for 67," Bryant snorted. "In other words, I'm most likely about to eat my last oyster with you boys."

With that, Bear slid another plump oyster out of its shell and down his throat. Then, with a wave, he turned and headed off for yet another pre-game press conference.

Lou Holtz was magnanimous in defeat.

"Coach Bryant, that's one fine team you've got there. A true champion," he said during the handshake at midfield.

"Thank you, Lou. And you're right. They're great young men. But I'm not sure they're two touchdowns better than your squad."

"I don't know, Coach. We played about as well as we could today."

"Well, you were good enough to make a tired old man want to go sit down and rest for a while," Bear said with a smile. He turned and headed away, but Holtz yelled for him to stop.

"Coach Bryant. Whoa! By the way, ..." Bear turned. "Good luck chasing Warner and Stagg."

Bryant nodded and smiled politely, but in all the confusion on the field and with the fans chanting his name up in the emptying Superdome bleachers, he couldn't figure out what in the world Lou Holtz was talking about.

The Sunday dinner dishes had been cleared. Mary Harmon and Paul Jr.'s wife, along with the grandaughters, were in the process of washing them. Bear and Paul Jr. had retired to the den to watch The Masters on television.

Just as they had the golf tournament dialed in, Bear turned down the volume.

"Son, I want to show you something interesting I noticed in our team press guide." He reached for the book and opened it. "See, this is what Lou Holtz was talking about when he wished me luck chasing down Mr. Warner and Mr. Stagg."

Paul Jr. shook his head.

"Papa, you mean you just realized you're going to win more college football games than any coach in history?"

"I didn't say that. Hell, I'm seventeen games away from tying Warner and eighteen away from tying Stagg. I might croak before I get close to either one of them."

"The magic number is 315."

The coach sat back in his easy chair.

"Goodness gracious! Where have the years gone?"

"You'll make it, Papa. It'll just take two more years at the rate you're going. Who knows? There might be a third straight national title this year."

Bear shook his head and half-watched one of the golfers tee off.

"I wouldn't count on that, Son. You know that super recruiting class we had last year? It's long in talent but short on discipline. I'm not sure these kids are willing to work as hard as it takes to win."

"What makes you think that?"

"Woody Hayes and I were talking about this in New Orleans a few years ago. Kids just have different priorities these days. I want players who love football as much as I do, and there aren't as many of those as there used to be. This team will need more motivating than any I've had before…and I'm not sure I've got enough left in me."

Bear kept his eyes on the television screen, but his son could tell his father was busy…already trying to figure out how he could get the most out of the young men who were just a few months away from pulling on the crimson jerseys, strapping on those helmets and going to war.

He had drawn up the same play a dozen times, wadded up the paper and tossed it into the wastepaper basket. He couldn't seem to get his mind on the work at hand. Then he heard the knock at the door he had been waiting for.

Gary White, his assistant in charge of keeping the players academically eligible, stepped through the door. Bear motioned for him to have a seat, while he picked up the phone and hit a button.

"Linda, hold all my calls until Gary and I finish. No exceptions. We've got some pitiful students to deal with." He hung up and looked at White. "Okay, partner, let's have some mid-term reports…something that's sure to put a damper on a 6-and-0 record and that win over Tennessee last week."

"Yes, sir. How do you want it?"

"Give me the worst first."

"That's too close to call, but I'd say…"

"Hey, I want to know the names of the players who aren't going to class or who aren't working hard enough once they get there. I'll take those right there on that couch at daybreak."

"And the others?"

"I'll let Coach Donahue work their asses off after practice."

The next morning, the coach was just finishing up his daily Bible reading and devotional study, right along with a cup of coffee. Across the desk from him stood a stocky young man, wearing jeans and a t-shirt, carrying a notebook and some textbooks. He looked sleepy. Sleepy and scared.

Bryant looked at his wristwatch, and then back at the player.

"Son, my watch says 6:10. That means you're ten minutes late."

"Yes, sir," he mumbled sleepily.

"Well, that's precisely the reason you're over here. You don't have any discipline."

The player shrugged and said, "I'm trying, Coach."

"Like hell you are! How are you going to learn anything if you don't go to class? How are you going to contribute to us winning if you don't pay the price?"

The player shrugged again.

"But I thought I was doing okay in football," he said.

"Hell, son, you're loafing! You're not in shape. We're about to win our 28th game in a row, and you haven't done one thing to help. And you've got twice as much ability as almost anybody else on our team."

"Coach, I'll help. I'll show you."

"Fine. But don't con yourself, because you sure can't con me. And you won't do a damn thing if you flunk out of school." Bear took a sip of coffee. "So, sit your ass down on that couch over yonder and start reading."

Bryant watched the player take a seat and open one of his textbooks, and then he eased back in his chair, picked up the Bible and began reading. He looked over the top of the Bible several times to make sure the player was still awake, still studying.

Finally, he said, "Young man, this is not a one-shot deal. You are going to see me right here every morning at 6 o'clock until your grades are good enough to suit me."

A few days later, before practice, Bear was about to start the climb up the ladder of his observation tower when one of his running backs trotted up beside him.

"Coach Bryant, I'd like to see you about something before we start."

"Of course, Joe."

The young man cleared his throat.

"As you know, we're about to go to Mississippi and play State."

"Uh huh. It's your day to play in front of the home folks."

The running back cleared his throat again and shifted from one foot to the other.

"Yes, sir, but what I was wondering is…well…when I was in high school, I wore one of these headbands under my helmet. You know, it was a trademark of mine."

"Uh huh."

"Well…I was wondering…could I start wearing this one…you know…sort of like those players at Oklahoma do?"

Bryant looked at the headband that the running back was holding and smiled.

"You know the rules, Joe. No facial hair and no uniform decoration." The coach's smile grew broader, and he put his hand on the young man's shoulder pad. "But I don't want to be hard-nosed about it. I'll make a deal with you, and you can decide. You can wear either the headband or the helmet. Not both. Not and play on this team."

The running back's eyes grew wide.

"Oh…then…I guess I'll wear a helmet."

Up in the broadcast booth, the Mississippi State network announcer was almost beside himself.

"How's this for drama?" the play-by-play man screamed. "The field goal team stays on the sideline. The number one team in the nation wants a touchdown for the win. Alabama is at the Bulldog three-yard line, and the Tide's having trouble hearing the snap count." Listeners could believe it. The roar on the radio from the metallic rattle of the cowbells in the stands was stunning. "There's the snap. Fumble! The ball is loose, and it looks like State has it! Yes, the Bulldogs have it! Mississippi State is going to win!"

The earthquake-like roar of the crowd confirmed it.

"State 6, Bama 3!" the announcer crowed. "The 28-game winning streak...the longest in the country...has been snapped. The Bulldogs have pulled off an unthinkable upset!"

Inside the dressing room, some of the players sobbed. Others pounded their lockers with their fists. One big tackle flung his helmet as hard as he could against the wall.

"Hey! That's enough of that," Bear said. "I don't ever want to see that again. Now, let's get our heads up and show some class. Let's be gracious in defeat like we've been while winning." He gazed around the room. He knew how bad they were hurting. So was he. "I don't want to hear any moaning and groaning about the crowd noise. We got whipped, pure and simple, so that won't do any good. That'll just leave a bad taste with everybody. Class. That's what I want to see. Learn something from this. Now, I'm going next door to congratulate the winning team.

"And if you see any of them outside, you do the same thing."

Chapter Fifteen:

A Record for the Masses

The Columnist watches from a distance but decides to wait a bit before interrupting them. He continues to hit balls down the driving range. Bear Bryant is hitting golf balls off the practice tee, as well. Billy Varner is with him, handing him a new ball after every swing.

Bear finally notices The Columnist.

"Billy, I believe that is Al down there at the other end," he says, plenty loud enough for The Columnist to hear him. "He didn't lie when he said he couldn't play golf worth a crap!"

The Columnist shoves his driver into his bag, picks it up and walks to where Bryant and Varner continue to send balls straight and true into the distance. Bear takes a moment before hitting the ball just as The Columnist steps up behind him.

"I better make this one a dandy because it'll most likely make the paper tomorrow morn-ing."

Varner laughs. "I think he has his notebook in his golf bag."

Bryant hits the ball solidly. It

goes far down the range and bounces out of sight right in the middle of the fairway.

The Columnist says, "I doubt Amos Alonzo Stagg could hit a golf ball like that. Pop Warner either."

Bryant watches the ball as long as he can see it.

"Nope, Alfred, but they could sure coach football, and they've given more to the game than I'll ever be able to."

"That's debatable, Coach. But what I'm wondering is what it'll really mean to you when you become the winningest football coach in history."

Bryant takes his time to hit another ball. It goes even farther than the last one did, and it flares just as straight and true. The Coach finally turns to face The Columnist and gives him that patented squint of his.

"You really want to talk about that bull now, Alfred?"

"Uh huh."

"Then let's at least go sit under that pine tree and get out of this hot sun."

They walk to the shade of the big pine, and all three men ease down to the cool grass. The coach leans back against the tree trunk and starts talking. The Columnist scribbles notes as fast as he can.

"It's not me. It's them…all those former players and assistant coaches. And everybody else I've been around. Like my mama, who I loved more than anybody. And my papa. Friends, too. Even my neighbors I've never talked to because I've been so damn busy. So, if the Lord blesses me some more…and he has already…it'll be a record for the masses, not for me."

"But coach," The Columnist pushes. "Won't you feel like you've done something special? Let's face it. To be number one is to be number one."

"Sure, Alfred. That's something I learned behind that plow, looking at the ass end of those mules. If you try something – planting corn, coaching football, even writing a newspaper column – you ought to try to be the very best you can be at it, or you're just wasting your time. I guess I've done my share of bringing new things to the game. Hell, the NCAA has had to double the size of their damned rulebook just to keep up with me…that tackle-eligible play old Jerry Duncan used to run for us…all these silly substitution rules…scholarship limits."

The Coach pauses to collect his thoughts, while The Columnist catches up with the shorthand marks on his notepad.

"Sure, Al, I've made an impact. But I'd be an absolute fool if I didn't acknowledge all the people who've helped me. Players like Pat Trammell and Steve Sloan and Ray Perkins. Babe Parilli. John David Crow. And that even goes for some folks I've never met…like Mr. Stagg and Mr. Warner. Without them, I might have never had the opportunity to be a football coach. Tell me, have you studied their careers?"

The Columnist nods. "Sure. Enough to know that Pop Warner used to have to urinate on the sideline during games because of bad kidneys."

Bryant chuckles deeply, and it causes a cough to flare up.

"Did he smoke as much as I do?"

"I don't know. But I somehow doubt it."

"Well, how about helping me get one more up on him. Let me bum a Marlboro."

The Columnist shakes his head as he reaches into his golf bag for a pack of cigarettes.

"I swear, Coach. You're a rich man who's trying to bust a poor man like me one cigarette at a time."

Bryant grins.

"Shit, Billy. Would you listen to that? I've given this one quotes that are worth thousands of dollars down through the years, and he's giving me a rough time over one little Marlboro."

The Columnist reaches to light the cigarette for the coach.

"And if you come up with nine wins this season, I'd appreciate you giving me a few more of 'em."

The coach winks, leans back against the tall pine and blows smoke toward the heavens.

"Coach Bryant, Steve Sloan is on the line," Linda Knowles called from his office doorway.

"That's exactly who I need to talk to," he replied and picked up the phone. "Hello, partner."

"Hey, Coach," Sloan said. "I'm calling because I've been worried about you. That tie with Southern Miss stunned me."

Bryant chewed on the end of his cigarette.

"Yeah, I know, but we haven't been sharp all season, really. I've got to believe that the players are feeling some pressure from this record hype everybody's talking about. So tell me, how would you handle that?"

Sloan chuckled. "Are you saying your prayers?"

"Uh huh. You doubting me?"

"That's good, and no, I'm not doubting you. I was just making sure you were on track."

"Oh, yeah. I'm talking to the good Lord bright and early every day. And Mary Harmon keeps me stocked with daily devotional materials. I've got one I'm gonna send you. It's called 'What Have I Traded for Today?' It's a reminder that every day is a gift from God, and that He expects some commitment in return."

Sloan clicked his tongue. "Maybe that's your answer. Maybe you need a little more commitment to get those five straight wins you need. And with…let's see…Tennessee, Rutgers, Mississippi State, Penn State and Auburn in front of you, maybe you ought to pray a little harder, too."

"Wouldn't hurt none at all to have a little divine help. Especially with Pat Dye down there at Auburn. It's gonna be tough. That man knows how to work and how to make his squad work just as hard as he does. I wish we could have kept him up here like I tried to do. But that's the way it is now. No easy wins on the schedule anymore, Steve. You got to scrap and fight and claw…and pray the good Lord favors you."

The small Alabama cheering section amid the sea of blue-clad Penn State fans screamed the words over and over: "Roll Tide! Roll Tide! Roll Tide!" And one wildly waved a sign with just three digits on it: "314."

Down on the field, Bear Bryant was dropped from the shoulders of his players at the corner of the field. As he trotted toward the locker room between two burly State Troopers, the crowd on either side and in the stands above seemed to form a friendly tunnel for them to run through. They were cheering for him, crying out for him to look up at them.

"Nice job, Bear!" one screamed.

"Just one more, Coach," another yelled.

"Pop is history! Now go get Stagg!" someone else bellowed.

Bryant turned to one of the Troopers.

"We've got the greatest folks in the world, coming all the way up here to follow us."

"Look again, Coach," the Trooper said. "It's theirs!"

The locker room in Birmingham was packed with cheering play-ers, happy coaches and cigar smoke. The players had handed their coach the game ball, and he stood there holding it, as if it might break if he should drop it.

"315! 315! 315!" the players chanted over and over.

Paul Bryant waved his free hand to try to quiet them down.

"Okay! That's enough. Listen! I've got something to say." The pandemonium slowly subsided enough so he could go on. "First, thank you for making an old man happy." The cheers gushed again. He waited a moment, then went on. "But more than anything, let me congratulate you on whipping Auburn. That was a hell of a show in the fourth quarter."

That set off another round of celebration. They only got quiet when they saw the manager moving toward Coach Bryant with a telephone in his hand.

"Coach Bryant, it's the president...calling from the White House."

Bryant took the phone but put the mouthpiece against his thigh so the president wouldn't hear him.

"Whatever we do, let's don't forget our team prayer." He raised the phone to his ear. "Hello, Gipper. How's everything up there in Washington?"

Chapter Sixteen:

Nothin' But a Winner

The banner that stretched across the front of the banquet hall in Washington, D.C. proclaimed this event to be "America's Tribute to Paul (Bear) Bryant." The room was filling fast for the pre-banquet cocktail party. It was already buzzing with conversation.

One of the early arrivals noticed the guest of honor and his wife in a far corner of the room, talking with someone they couldn't quite see.

"Who in the hell is that with Bear and Mary Harmon?" he asked his buddy.

"I don't know, but the son of a bitch has them cornered for some serious conversation, don't he?"

Another man standing nearby couldn't help but overhear the exchange. He tapped the first speaker on the shoulder.

"Gentlemen, you might want to rephrase some of that," he said.

"Why?"

"Because that man they're talking to is the Reverend Billy
Graham."

"Oh, shit," the man said.

At that moment, Bear Bryant
was saying, "Dr. Graham, I don't
know why God chose a sinner

like me to have such a wonderful life, but I'm most appreciative."

"Thankful, Paul," Mary Harmon corrected. "You're thankful for a blessing, appreciative of friends."

Dr. Graham laughed.

"Either way is okay, Mary Harmon. What matters is that your husband is much more serious about his spiritual life than a lot of people think he is."

Bryant smiled.

"I hope that means I'm not going to hell."

Mary Harmon cuffed him on the shoulder and said, "Paul William Bryant!"

But Reverend Graham was looking the old football coach directly in the eye when he said, "Actually, Coach, I'd say wings have been reserved for you."

The ice cream piled on the slice of birthday cake had already melted. Mary Harmon checked the clock on the kitchen wall and told her son, "I wouldn't keep Cherrie and the girls waiting too long. They've got school tomorrow."

Paul Jr. checked his own wristwatch.

"Mama, I think I'm going to walk home."

"What's wrong?"

"I'm just wondering what's eating at Papa. He just wasn't himself tonight. I know he hates birthdays, but at least he usually puts on a show for the kids. He didn't even try tonight."

He didn't miss the worried look on his mother's face. So she had noticed it, too.

"I know," she said. "I'll talk to him tonight, so I'll have a report for you tomorrow." She considered the wrinkles on the backs of her hands. "Maybe it's just number sixty-nine with seventy looming right ahead."

She waited until her husband was ready for bed, sitting in a chair in their bedroom, smoking a cigarette and finishing up his newspaper. He looked up when she came into the room.

"Can I help you, ma'am?"

"No, thank you, but maybe I can help you." She sat down on the bed near him. "What's the problem?"

"Nothing."

"Come on, it's not like we just started dating last week."

He slammed down the newspaper.

"That's right. And just remember that you're almost as old as I am."

"So that's what's got you all…"

"That's right. And I bet you feel a hell of a lot better than me."

She waited until he had calmed back down, then said, "Let's go out to the kitchen and get a glass of milk. Maybe another piece of your birthday cake."

It was such a familiar scene, the two of them sitting at the table, talking over late-night glasses of milk. She knew he would finally open up to her there. And she was right.

"So that's how it is," he was saying. "I'm cold when it's a hundred degrees at practice. And there are times when I don't have enough damn energy to blow the whistle. I'm over the hill. And I've got a team that's going to go down like the Titanic."

"Well, Paul, do what the doctor says. Get off those Chesterfields."

"He said I should walk more and worry a lot less."

"Good advice! There's nothing to worry about. The team looked great, the way they beat Tech and Ole Miss."

He picked up his milk but didn't take a drink.

"That's just two out of eleven, Sugar. And I'm telling you right now, Auburn and LSU are better than we are, and Tennessee is due. We're not nearly as strong as people think. That means some long streaks are going to come to an end." He set down his glass and wrapped his arms across his chest. "And me, too, if I don't turn around this chilling."

The announcers for the Alabama Radio Network were summing up the game, the outcome obvious in their heavy voices.

"Well, another season of great promise is slipping away," one said. "The final score: LSU 20, Alabama 10. The Crimson Tide just doesn't look like itself."

"That's true," confirmed his partner. "We did put up a heck of a fight before losing by a touchdown at Tennessee, but today, well, it was all Bengal Tigers from the kickoff. Even more so than the scoreboard indicates."

"It's amazing that this Alabama team was ranked number two in the country after five wins to start the season. But even back then, Coach Bryant seemed worried that he wouldn't be able to keep a fire built under his players."

Downstairs in the press room, Coach Bryant was, at that moment, addressing the gathered reporters from behind a bank of microphones. The room was eerily quiet as the coach talked slowly and deliberately, as if the words were hard to push out.

"So today, I'm suggesting the school conducts a full review of our football program. And it should start at the top. That's where I sit." A couple of the writers chuckled, and several exchanged knowing glances. They didn't believe a word of it. "I'm serious about this. I've given it a lot of thought. You see, I'm for Alabama. And Alabama deserves a coach who can keep it moving forward, not backward like I have the last two months."

After the press conference, a gaggle of reporters were waiting at the elevator, ready to head out to file their stories.

"Well, John, what about it?" one of them asked another. "Do you think he's serious about leaving this time?"

"Why, hell no!" the second reporter scoffed. "He's said the same junk before, when times got tough."

"Yeah, but look how long that's been. Twelve years."

The elevator doors opened then, and they all stepped onboard. As the doors eased shut, the second reporter said, "It'd take a damn fool to believe him. He's just trying to fire up the troops and get them…"

But the elevator was gone.

The Columnist sits in a booth at a restaurant, drinking whiskey and water. Across from him, sipping his own whiskey, is the new sports information director at the University of Alabama, Jack Perry.

Perry has his head cocked in disbelief as he talks with The Columnist.

"So, you don't have any doubts about this, Al?"

"Nope. He's leaving. And I'm telling you because his sports information director has to be prepared for something this big."

Perry takes a big gulp of his drink.

"I don't doubt your opinion. But exactly what was it he said to you after the press conference?"

The Columnist sips his own drink before repeating what he has told Perry twice already.

"I said, 'You're serious, aren't you?' and he said, 'Yep, Alfred, the time has come.'"

Perry nods. He is convinced.

"So I guess I'll play dumb, wait for him to direct me but be ready for all hell to break loose."

"That'll work," The Columnist says and drains the last of the liquid from his glass. "As for me, I've got a few things to get off my chest with him...and Jack, he isn't going to like it. I just hope he favors the honesty."

It is not easy for The Columnist to lecture someone the stature of Bear Bryant. It's early, just after dawn. Bear, seated behind his desk, has his Bible open and his daily devotional material arrayed around it. The Columnist, standing before the desk, has no choice, though. He has something he wants to say, and he says it.

"I asked for three minutes, so I guess I've overstayed already. But Coach, it just doesn't add up...you talking about quitting while your team is getting its ass beat. Hell, you're the man who has always told players that football is training them for those days when their houses burn down, their children are sick, and their wives have left for other men. All of those tough times that will come later in their lives. And now you're quitting on them in their darkest hour."

Bryant leans back in his chair.

"Do you feel better now?" he asks The Columnist.

"Yes, sir. And I apologize for taking so long."

"Take a seat, Alfred," Bryant says, motioning toward one of the chairs in front of the big desk. The coach stands, unbuttons his right shirtsleeve at the wrist and rolls it up past the elbow. The arm is badly swollen and an ugly dark blue color, as if it is badly bruised. "This is why I have to quit, Alfred. My doctor said I'm moving toward a stroke if I don't get out now." The Columnist drops his head. He had no idea. "Don't worry about it. I appreciate you saying what you did. But it's been fifty years, Alfred. Fifty years of football. Fifty years of nothing else. Isn't that enough time for a man to give to one thing?"

The Columnist looks up.

"Yes, sir. As long as he doesn't have anything left to give."

Bryant leans forward, inadvertently putting his hand on the open

Bible. He looks tired, older than he actually is. There's a weakness in his eyes The Columnist has never seen before.

"Alfred, I might have a little more left to give. I really might. But I'm at a point now where I can't."

He wore a bright red sport coat with a tie. No hat, of course. He never wore a hat inside…not even when he played in the Superdome. He said his mama told him to never wear a hat in the house.

The room was amazingly quiet, considering how many reporters and others were crowded inside and how many cameras were aimed his direction.

He reached inside his coat pocket and removed a piece of paper. When he read, it sounded halting, almost forced, as if he was having trouble making out the words on the paper.

"There comes a time in every profession when you need to hang it up, and that time has come for me as head football coach at the University of Alabama." He ignored the flash of several cameras, the just-audible gasp from the assembled writers, even though they knew the reason they had been summoned to this place this morning. "My main purpose as director of athletics and head football coach has been to field the best possible team, to improve each player as a person and to produce citizens who will be credits to our modern-day society. We have been successful in most of those areas, but now I feel the time is right for a change in our football leadership."

Bear's secretary, Linda Knowles, and his bodyguard, Billy Varner, were seated in the audience. Knowles was crying, slowly shaking her head from side to side. The reporters scratched away on their pads, trying not to miss a word.

"We lost two big football games this year that we should have

won, four in all. And we played only four or five games like a
Bryant-coached team should. I've done a poor job of coaching. This
is my school, my alma mater, and I love it. And I love the players.
But in my opinion, they deserve better coaching than they've been
getting from me this year. I'm stepping down in an effort to see that
they get better coaching from someone else." He paused then and
looked up from the sheet of paper from which he had been reading.
"As for me, I'm a tired old man who has one more bowl game to
coach. But I'm not tired of football. And friends, I don't guess I ever
will be."

The room was deathly quiet. Everyone had a stunned look on his
face. A few of the hard-boiled reporters even had tears in their eyes.

It was a long moment before they finally all stood and hurried off
to file the story they had known was coming but still never imag-
ined they would ever write.

It is a sunny day, unseasonably warm for December in
Tuscaloosa. Bear Bryant is on his throne, high atop his observation
tower, watching his squad work out on the brown grass field below.

It is his last practice on Thomas Field, the football practice facility at the University of Alabama.

On a bench at the base of the tower, The Columnist sits with
another sportswriter, John Pruett, and Pruett's ten-year-old son.

Atop the tower, Bryant blows his whistle for the final time.

"Okay, okay, okay! That should do it. Let's huddle up and get
ready to go to the Liberty Bowl. Let's get ready to beat Illinois."

The players break into a spirited cheer as they jog to the middle
of the field while their coach climbs down from the tower one last
time and ambles out to join them.

Pruett turns to The Columnist.

"I'd give anything to be out there listening to this," he says.

"What do you think he's saying, Dad?" his son asks.

"I don't know, but you can bet those players will remember every word of it."

The Columnist watches the big huddle in the middle of the field, feels the surprisingly mild breeze blowing across from the general direction of the football stadium and sees the sun quickly falling out of sight back beyond the University.

"I'll remember this setting for a long time," The Columnist says, his voice breaking slightly.

"Yep. And Laddie, now we've got to find out what he's thinking," Pruett says. There are readers who will want to know, of course.

The two men and the boy catch up with the coach as he heads off the practice field. Bear nods to the newspapermen but takes an interest in the boy.

"John, my little friend here is growing up in a hurry," he says.

"Yes, sir, much too fast to suit me. But I guess that's the way life goes."

"Uh huh. And there will be a million memories along the way."

The Columnist turns to look at the coach.

"I expect you're feeling a few right about now," he says.

"A bunch of 'em. Most of them good. And they keep coming." He nodded back toward the broad expanse of discolored grass behind them, the field chewed up by the cleats of the players. "I guess I've spent a jillion hours on this field, either as a player or as a coach. And I've seen what must be a million faces." His step had slowed, as if he might be hesitant to step off this hallowed ground once and for all. "Coach Thomas. Coach Hank. Coach Drew. Howell and Hutson. Pat Trammell. Joe and Lee Roy. And all those others who've allowed us to be winners. They're Alabama football, men. Not Paul Bryant. They're the ones who matter. And to whom I'm indebted."

Then, the coach steps into the tunnel beneath the street that runs between the practice field and Memorial Coliseum and is gone.

Behind them, the sun is almost down and it will soon be dark.

There is nothing else quite like the final few moments in a football locker room – the final minutes before a big game. The smell of liniment and sweat, the scratch of cleats on the floor, the nervous coughs, the last-minute whispered instructions or words of encouragement.

The pre-game pep talk by the coach is often over-emphasized, too. It is usually little more than a short speech, reminding the players of what all is at stake and urging them to get out there and do what they've been taught to the best of their abilities.

Bear had said it himself many times. Games aren't won because of the pep talk or any last-minute words of inspiration from the coach. By the last few moments before the kickoff, "the hay is in the barn."

Still, on this cold night in Memphis, he knew this speech was different. Sure, it was his last. But he also felt he owed this group of young men something: an apology.

He paced among them as he spoke.

"Gentlemen, I want to thank you for what you've gone through the last month or so. And some of you have had to put up with a bunch of senseless distractions for the past two years. I apologize for that. And I'm proud of the way you've handled it. Class…that's the Alabama way, and it's what separates you from a lot of others who aren't fortunate enough to wear those crimson war bonnets."

Several of the players looked at the helmets they held in their laps.

"Now let's talk about this game," he continued. "The first thing I want to say is you've got to forget about me and go play this game for yourselves, for your teammates and for your school. For your mamas and papas, too, as well as all the other relatives, your classmates and friends. But gentlemen, mostly you've got to play this game for you." He pointed an outstretched finger around the room, aimed at the young men who sprawled on the floor or lay back inside their lockers. He smiled then, and said, "This isn't my last game. It's your next game. And you owe it to yourself to do your best on every play."

He paused then. Took off his baseball cap. Seemed on the verge of getting emotional. The players sensed it. Sensed the turmoil that must be roiling inside the old coach at that moment.

"In summary, men" he finally said, "you've to go out there and hold up your heads and…"

He stopped then, pausing for a longer time as his voice cracked. His lip trembled. The players looked away, wishing they could help him through this awkward moment.

The old coach's eyes were misty but, when he spoke again, his voice was as strong as it ever was.

"It's yours to win, not mine. It's your pride on the line out there tonight, not mine. And I'll be proud of you, win or lose, because you're special. You're special because you play for Alabama."

Then, there it was. A large tear rolled from one eye, down his cheek, followed by another.

"Go out there and win this game for yourselves, gentlemen. After all, you'll have to live with this game a long time after I'm gone."

Epilogue

Alabama defeated Illinois in that Liberty Bowl game by a score of 21-15. It was played on December 29, 1982. He told friends that he was just a tired old man who had never gotten tired of football.

On January 26, 1983 – only four weeks later – Paul "Bear" Bryant was pronounced dead at Druid City Hospital in Tuscaloosa, Alabama, about a mile from the Thomas Field football practice facility at the University. He was the victim of a stroke and heart problems.

Bryant coached 323 victories, 232 of which came while he was head coach at the University of Alabama.

Legendary Nebraska coach Bob Devaney said, "He was simply the best there ever was."

Penn State Coach Joe Paterno, who, along with Florida State's Bobby Bowden, later broke Bryant's winning record, said, "Even his peers in the coaching business felt in awe of him. He had such great charisma. He was just a giant figure."

Paul Bryant was universally recognized to be not only a great football coach but also a man of great commitment and class, and a gifted motivator of men.

And he was, all the way through his final game, nothing but a winner.